CUSTOMER
SERVICE
RENAISSANCE

CUSTOMER SERVICE
RENAISSANCE

Lessons from the
Banking Wars

M. RAY GRUBBS & R. ERIC REIDENBACH

BANKERS PUBLISHING COMPANY
PROBUS PUBLISHING COMPANY
Chicago, Illinois

This publication is designed to provide accurate and authoritative information in regard to the subject matter covered. It is sold with the understanding that the publisher is not engaged in rendering legal, accounting or other professional service.

Library of Congress Number: 91-62344

ISBN 1-55738-321-9

Contents

List of Figures

Preface

The banking industry can be characterized in any number of different ways. One way that captures the nature of the current competitive situation is to describe the industry as a commodity industry. It is comprised of a large and growing number of undifferentiated competitors, selling an undifferentiated product for which there are many substitutes. Adding to this characterization is a belief on the part of many bank managements that the major form of competition is price based.

The truth is that bank managements have a greater degree of control over their competitive situation than many believe. The major competitive weapon is customer service. It is, after all, the only patent protection they have. There is no doubt that outstanding customer service is the number one strategic priority for many banks during the 1990s. Because of its importance, we have researched a number of different banking organizations in terms of their service delivery system with the purpose of finding those banks that can serve as models of outstanding service deliverers. Our research involved talking to customers, interviewing different banks about their programs, and spending countless hours reading about innovative service strategies. From this research we have focused on four banks that use customer service to achieve four different strategies.

We begin with a community bank and then proceed to a commercial bank, a bank that uses customer service as a full distribution strategy for all its 183 branches, and a bank that caters only to upscale clientele. Each bank has something to offer the manager eager to learn about customer service. It is our hope that you will find the different banks as useful models to provide a basis for fine tuning or implementing your own version of customer service. In a sense, each chapter becomes a blueprint for developing or honing your own particular version of customer service.

But, perhaps the most important lesson that customer service driven organizations have learned is the importance of listening to their customers. Because this customer driven concept of service is so critical to the success of these top service organizations, we want to revisit some of the key points customers told us about what top-notch service means to them. Special chapters are included which will allow you to listen in on the conversations about customer service as told to us by banking customers across the country.

Finally, we conclude the book with a summary chapter that will draw together some of the basic lessons in developing and implementing customer service strategies for the banking industry. We hope this book will put your bank on the road to becoming the customer service leader in your market.

Acknowledgments

The individuals you will read about in this book have all been extremely cooperative and helpful. It is our hope that we have adequately depicted their effort, innovative spirit, and genius. Special thanks to Ms. Jane Hill, Secretary in the Center for Business Development and Research at the University of Southern Mississsippi for her help and support. It was invaluable.

Chapter

What the Early Battles Have Taught Us

Some Mixed News from the Customer Service Front

No other industry has undergone such fundamental changes in such a short time as has the commercial banking industry. During this brief period of massive convulsion, bank managements have had to learn as they battled. The industry has been attacked on numerous fronts, ranging from credit card companies, automobile companies, credit unions, S&Ls, retailers, insurance companies, telephone and communication companies, to brokerage houses. The result is a battlefield littered by those banks that have been unable, for one reason or another, to adjust to this new type of warfare. Those, however, that remain strong and competitive have learned a number of lessons from these early battles. *Perhaps the most important lesson learned is that the customer is*

1

the single most important part of banking and that customer service is a fundamental strategic requirement for growth and survival. This is a universal message for any business person in any type of organization.

The importance of customer service has been a hard learned lesson for many bankers who have been used to dealing with the customer on their own terms, rather than on the customer's terms. What many in the banking industry have called "an inside order taker mentality" has died hard. As we reported earlier in our book *Winning Banks: Managing Service Quality for Customer Satisfaction* (Rolling Meadows, Illinois: Bank Administration Institute, 1989), banking has had a very poor reputation concerning its delivery of customer service. Customers have told us that doing business with their bank is like "doing the dishes" or "fixing a flat tire" or "cleaning the bathroom." In nationwide focus groups conducted for the Bank Administration Institute, one customer summed up the attitude of many others by saying, "Banking can never be a positive experience. You just hope that it will not be too negative."

In *Winning Banks* we reported that in a national survey consumers gave commercial banks a very poor service rating, ranking them below such firms as supermarkets, restaurants, hotels, and department stores. Ten years later another national survey shows that there has been little improvement in the service rating of the commercial banking industry. In a *Wall Street Journal/ NBC News* poll, 29% of the respondents said the service they receive from their bank is "getting worse." About half indicated it was "about the same" with only 17% indicating some improvement. This places banks, as an industry, behind businesses such as supermarkets, automobile dealerships, restaurants, department stores, and hotels. The good news, if you want to call it that, is that the commercial banking industry leads the airlines, insurance companies, and gas stations in the level of service offered to its customers.[1] With a customer base holding these types of attitudes, it is no wonder competitors have been able to establish such secure and strong beachheads. All they had to do to win banking customers away from the commercial banking industry was to promise them that they would be treated the way they wanted to be treated, as *valued customers.*

What we see now in the industry is a customer service renaissance, a rebirth of the recognition that the customer is the fundamental element in the banking relationship. With that comes the realization that to win and maintain customer relationships, organizations can no longer treat them with indifference. Unfortunately, this recognition is not always translated into programs and actions which communicate quality customer service. Impeding the clear translation of thought to action is a hesitancy or inability on the part of many bank managements to establish customer service as a fundamental strategic option. At the heart of this problem is a misunderstanding of the value of a top quality customer service strategy and how it can benefit an organization. Let's examine, in some detail, what we have learned about customer service as a strategic option since *Winning Banks* was first published in 1989. Why should your bank or business become a top quality service deliverer?

Lesson 1: Customer Service Expectations Are High and Getting Higher

There is little doubt that consumers are expecting and getting a higher quality of service from business than they did before. American industry has learned that to be competitive in the domestic and international marketplace, they must deliver top notch products and first rate customer service. Ford Motor Company has been promising the American public that at Ford, "Quality is job one" and we are now seeing signs that they are delivering on their quality promise. Other companies like Seattle based Nordstroms Department Store, American Express, Marriott Hotels, Delta Airlines, Johnson & Johnson, Bugs Burger Bug Killers (a Miami based extermination company), and a host of other well run customer driven companies are teaching customers that they can get better service. In a 1990 survey of 534 executives by Paul Ray and Carre Orban International, respondents were asked, "What company do you believe sets the standard for service quality in America?" Topping the list was IBM, followed by Nordstroms, American Express, AT&T, McDonald's, Federal Express, Walt Disney, General Electric, Marriott, American Airlines, L. L. Bean, Delta Airlines, Xerox, and Wal-Mart. Not one bank was mentioned![2]

We have experienced some legendary examples of customer service that people are experiencing throughout their interactions with business. Customer service drives employee interactions with customers at the Marriott Hotels. At a meeting of bankers in Atlanta, Georgia, one of the authors was looking for a conference room in which he was to make a presentation. As I was wandering around the bottom floor of this cavernous hotel looking lost and harried, a maintenance man carrying a ladder stopped and asked if he could help. "I'm looking for the conference room in which the banker's group is meeting," I said. The maintenance man put down the ladder and took me to the room. Clearly, that is not in his job description, but nevertheless it was an opportunity to provide service to the customer, a value that most of the Marriott people exhibit. Marriott is frequently referred to as an example of a company that really provides top notch customer service.

We often hear about the high level of service that people receive from Delta Airlines. On a return trip from Latin America we experienced what customer service means at Delta. I was travelling with a companion who was suffering from a residual of exotic cuisine enjoyed the previous night in San Salvador, El Salvador. We had trouble leaving El Salvador and, while our destination was New Orleans, our only chance to leave was via Los Angeles. We arrived in Los Angeles at 1:30 AM after travelling all day and went to Delta to book a flight from Los Angeles to New Orleans. We asked for first class seats since we were tired and not feeling well. The Delta representative said that Delta did not offer first class on this flight but that American did. *Not only did she recommend another airline, but she made the reservations for us!* Delta lost business in the short run but has gained two very loyal customers who will spend much more money flying Delta. Now when we book a flight we give Delta the first call.

This expectation of high quality service that customers are receiving from Delta, Marriott Hotels, and other companies is carried over to the relationships customers have with their bank. If customers can get quick and responsive service from a hamburger place, why can't they get quick responsive service from their bank? If employees at a waffle house can be trained to give an effusive and warm reception to a customer, why can't bank employees demonstrate this same eagerness and drive? If an exterminator can deliver on a promise of a bug free environment, why can't a bank provide competent service? The commercial banking industry is being forced to improve its service delivery systems because other businesses are setting high standards and expectations. The banking industry has a choice. It can either join in the customer service renaissance or face the consequences. *Customer service is the number one strategic priority for the 1990s!*

Lesson 2: High Quality Customer Service Can Reduce Costs

Perhaps the most often heard complaint by bank management is that high quality customer service costs too much. In the short run, there is a cost to initiate a customer service strategy. To become a top deliverer of customer service does require an upfront investment on the part of a bank. This additional expenditure runs head on into an industry concerned with cost containment and downsizing. But bank managements must not confuse long-term objectives with short-term expediences. In the longer run, bank managements must embrace a "customer first, banking second" mentality. And, there is significant evidence that once the short-run costs of becoming a high quality service delivery system are absorbed, good customer service can actually save money.

Consider my experience in attempting to open a checking account at a local bank. As a customer, I walked in and was greeted by a delightful woman asking if she could help me. I explained that I wanted to open a checking account and she identified my options. I settled on a basic checking account with a $2 service charge per month. She then asked me the questions on the application form and, once completed, told me my checks would be delivered to my house within ten days. I was given five counter checks with my new account number typed on them.

After ten days no checks had arrived. I waited another couple days and finally went back to the bank. I was greeted by another woman and I told her my problem. She told me she would have to check with her branch manager. The branch manager came out of her office and asked me what the *problem* was. I told her the same thing I had told the woman. Finally, the branch manager told the woman to take another application. She did and told me that my checks would be delivered to my house within ten days. Upon leaving, I asked if I could have some more checks since I had used the initial five during the previous two weeks. The woman explained to me that it was against the *policy* of the bank to give more checks. I asked her to get the branch manager. I explained to the branch manager that I had used up my five checks and that I needed more. The branch manager explained that the bank did not like to give out counter checks, but, in this case would make an exception. Ten days later, my checks arrived. I opened the box and read the statement asking me to examine the checks for accuracy. I did so and found that my name was misspelled. I went back to the bank and closed my half-opened account.

The point of this story is how much did it cost the bank to open a basic checking account? How much should it have cost them? If the bank had handled the transaction in a more competent and responsive manner they might still have the business. These are soft dollar costs that need not be incurred.

Here's another example of a cost avoidance situation that could have saved a bank some money. A woman had her check book stolen with only two checks remaining. She notified her "personal banker" immediately and told him of the theft and the numbers on the stolen checks. Unfortunately, unknown to the woman, someone was asleep at the switch and her bank cashed the checks. Meanwhile, the woman wrote a check for $600 for a purchase, believing that the money was in her account. The check was returned NSF. After two days of bureaucratic hassle with several different "personal bankers" the bank found itself out the $600 and a good customer.

A lack of competency on the part of bank personnel can be an expensive proposition. *We do not know of a single task in banking or any business that costs less when it has to be done two or more times instead of being done right the first time.* Recovery costs tend to account for a significant portion of a bank's operating costs, attesting to the cost of "unquality service."

Lesson 3: Loyal Customers Buy and Don't Have to Be Sold

How much is a loyal customer worth? Tom Peters, author of *In Search of Excellence*, estimates that a smaller account represents $180,000 worth of business over a ten-year period and a single patron of an upscale grocery will spend $50,000 over that same time period.[3]

Similarly, John Goodman of TARP (Technical Assistance Research Programs) estimates that an automobile dealer can count on $150,000 worth of business from a loyal customer, while appliance makers can expect about $30,000 in sales over a 20 year period from their loyal customers.[4]

Loyal customers are a source of "efficient revenues." Efficient revenues mean that the cost of generating revenues from loyal customers is less than the cost of acquiring new customers; they are more profitable. Why? Essentially, *loyal customers buy and don't have to be sold.* The marketing effort necessary to generate revenues from loyal customers is significantly less than that associated with trying to attract, persuade, and sell new customers. This point was brought home to us by an elderly woman in Chicago. In a series of focus groups that formed the basis of *Winning Banks* we asked the question, "Would you buy this $6 a month package account from your bank?" One group participant explained the importance of customer service in her decision by saying, "Why should I pay $6 a month for crappy service when I can get it for $2?" That, is a hard selling proposition! Loyal customers buy more and are easier to sell. *When you are selling service and have done a poor job of meeting customer expectations in the past, why would you expect customers to pay for more poor service? Would you pay more for poor service?*

Luke Helms, CEO of Seattle based Seafirst Bank, estimates that it costs his bank, "five times as much to bring in a new customer as it does to keep an established one."[5] In fact, a marketing rule of thumb pegs the cost of customer acquisition at about three to five times the cost of customer retention. Many businesses understand what Helms is talking about and focus their training efforts on customer retention, because loyal customers buy more, give good positive word of mouth advertising, and are willing to pay higher prices.

MBNA of America, the parent of Maryland National Bank and the credit card operation of Baltimore based MNC Financial, manages to hold onto 95% of its customers while nationally, companies experience a customer turnover of about 20%. The reason for their strong customer allegiance is found in the high level of customer service they offer. What prompted this focus on customer retention and customer service? Charles Crawley, President of MBNA found out that, "a new card member costs him $100 to acquire but a five-year customer brings in an average $100 in profits annually, and a ten-year cardholder produces $300."[6]

Lesson 4: Poor Service Is the Number One Reason for Customer Defections

Couple this cost of customer acquisition with what we know about why retail bank customers leave their bank. Studies we conducted indicate that 25% of customers who close an account with a bank do so because of poor customer service. Other studies indicate that this figure might be as high as 42%. Moreover, surveys by Raddon Financial Group estimate that each closed account, on average, means the loss of a three product relationship and a deposit balance of $23,000.[7]

The research conducted by Seafirst Bank indicates similar findings regarding customer switching. Their research found that 68% of the switchers cited an attitude of indifference toward the customer as the reason for leaving the bank, 14% indicated product dissatisfaction, 9% gave competition as a reason, 5% said that they had developed other banking relationships, 3% moved away, and 1% died. Regardless of what studies you look at, the message is clear. *Overall, the number one reason customers give for switching banks is poor customer service.*

Lesson 5: Negative Word of Mouth Destroys Promotional Returns

Consider for a moment how much your bank is spending on promotion-advertising and other promotional efforts aimed at developing an image of solid customer service. Now take a look at what happens when you don't deliver on your promise of service: The average dissatisfied customer will tell a disparaging story about his or her experience at your bank to at least nine other people. We also know that an additional 13% of dissatisfied customers will gripe about their negative experience to an additional 20 people. Now, consider that only about 2% of dissatisfied customers ever complain to management.

Let's put this into perspective. Assume that you are handling one complaint per month or twelve a year. This represents the 2% that management is aware of. That means that there is a potential of 600 dissatisfied customers out there telling people about the way they were treated in your bank. If the average dissatisfied customer tells his or her story to nine other people (9 x 600 = 5400) and 13% tell an additional 20 (600 x .13 = 78 x 20 =1560), *then all told, a potential of 6,960 people are hearing negative stories about your bank.* The devastating aspect of negative publicity is that it is a much more credible source of information than your advertising is. Customers will tend to believe their friends and neighbors more readily than they will your ads.

In working with banks we have found that a number of bank managements think that they can short circuit the customer service strategy by simply advertising greater customer service without going through the necessary work of making sure that they are in deed, as well as in word, customer service driven. Not only does this approach not work, but we find that it usually creates additional problems for bank managements.

Running ads telling people that customer service is a driving force at your bank, when it is not, only creates perceptions and expectations that the bank cannot meet. Customer satisfaction is the difference between what customers expect and their perceptions of what they actually receive. Customers are satisfied when what they receive is greater than or equal to what they expect. Driving customer expectations high and then not delivering on those expectations will only guarantee a dissatisfied customer and add to the number of upset customers spreading negative publicity about your bank.

Advertising what they could not deliver proved to be a costly mistake for Florida Power & Light Company. Throughout the 1980s, FP&L had sold itself as "a master of quality control" to its customers. Unfortunately, a statewide freeze last Christmas exposed the claim to reality. Unable to supply enough power, FP&L incurred the wrath of its customers.

Leading Edge found itself in the same situation. The darlings of the computer world, the maker of IBM clones, had offered a 15-month guarantee—a full 12 months longer than any other manufacturer. Unfortunately, an ill-conceived diversification drained cash reserves and distorted management attention resulting in an inability to fulfill orders. Repairs could not be effected and Leading Edge's customers could not rely on the company. "When I start pumping up people's service expectations and don't deliver, I end up giving worse service than if I had never said anything at all," offers William H. Davidow, co-author of *Total Customer Service.*[8]

Lesson 6: Quality Service Means Greater Pricing Freedom

Winning Banks talked about the commodity trap and how many bank managements have unwittingly managed their institutions into a loss of image and loss of control over the bank's pricing policies. The commodity trap results when a bank's management fails to recognize those aspects of the bank which can make it unique, those aspects that can give the bank a specific, identifiable image. It is a failure of creative management. Too often, bank managements take the view that what they are offering the public is no different from another financial institution and, therefore, the only way to attract and keep customers is through price competition. When this management malaise sets in and prices are cut, it sets in motion a series of events wherein reduced margins force additional cost cuts. These cuts usually are effected by reductions in the numbers of employees which, in turn, reduces the level of customer service that the bank provides its market. When a number of banks embark upon this self-destructing price competitive strategy, customers begin to see banking as a commodity business, wherein no bank is different from the other, and that the only reason to choose a particular bank is because that bank is offering the lowest prices.

Corn, hog bellies, cotton, ball bearings, and chickens are examples of commodities. There is no loyalty to a producer of a commodity. The product lacks differentiation so consequently one chicken is usually as good as another. And, in a commodity situation, the producer has no control over the price he or she charges for the product.

The point we made in *Winning Banks* and the point we wish to make again now, is simply, *there need be no such thing as a commodity in the banking business.*

Earlier we mentioned an extermination company called Bugs Burger Bug Killers (BBBK).[9] This is a Miami based company that was recently bought out by Johnson's Wax. BBBK is no ordinary exterminator. They charge four times what their competitors charge and they carry about 9 to 12% profit on sales in an industry that traditionally brings about 5% to their bottom line. The extermination business, by most descriptions, is a commodity business. It was, until BBBK came along. Customers tended to view one bug killer the same as another. What is it about

BBBK that allows it to charge higher prices and make more money? What is it that has allowed BBBK to avoid the commodity trap and stand out from the crowd?

The answer lies in their value-added approach to doing business. BBBK adds value through a high level of customer service. For example, at BBBK you do not pay for an initial clean out and monthly service until you agree that BBBK's swat team has destroyed all nesting and breeding places on your premises. Only then do you begin to pay for their services. If the bug guys can't maintain a clean premise you will receive a refund for your last 12 months (they obviously count heavily on competent people), plus free service for a year from the exterminator of your choice. If a hotel or restaurant guest sees a roach, BBBK pays the guest for his meal or room, writes a letter of apology and then issues a gift certificate for a future room or meal. BBBK understands the idea of adding value to their commodity-like product with heavy doses of customer service. *In so doing they are able to differentiate themselves from their competition, charge a higher price, be more profitable, and above all stay out of the commodity trap.*

Another commodity-like business that understands the value of customer service is Premier Industrial Corporation, a distributor of industrial parts. Several years ago, the manager of a Caterpillar tractor plant in Decatur, Illinois called Premier to locate a $10 electrical relay. The relay had broken down and forced the stoppage of work on one of Caterpillar's assembly lines. A part was located in a Los Angeles warehouse and was rushed to a plane bound for St. Louis. By 10:30 PM that same night, the part was delivered by a Premier employee much to the appreciation of the Caterpillar manager. There is no doubt that Premier pays extra to provide this type and quality of service, but the rewards are outstanding. "Premier can charge up to 50% more than competitors for every one of the 250,000 mundane industrial parts it stocks, and its return on equity was a healthy 27.8% on sales of $596 million in 1989. In its latest fiscal year, Premier earned a 32.2% ROE (three times industry average) and a ROA of 25% (about four times industry average)."[10]

This same profitability is found in another top notch service deliverer, Delta Airlines. Delta's actual fiscal 1990 net leads the industry. Delta's net profit margin for 1990 was 3.5% compared to 1.1% for American, 2.7% for United and .5% for the entire airline industry.[11] Co-founder and Chairman of Premier, Morton L. Mandel explains, "To us customer service is the main event."[12] These thoughts are echoed by Roger Enrico, President of Pepsi-Co Worldwide Beverages, who summarizes his business philosophy, "If you are totally customer-focused and you deliver the services your customers want, everything else will follow."[13]

Once in the commodity trap, climbing out is not easy. Ask the management of Continental Airlines. Climbing out of Chapter 11 requires Continental to attract and retain business travelers. This may not be easy for Continental. A poll published last year revealed that only 9% of this market indicated a preference for Continental. The plan? Continental, once known as a major discounter, must shed its commodity wings, offer more and better services and maintain high morale among its employees. In short, add value to its product. A two-day customer service seminar and additional expenditures on preparing 25,000 employees for its new image have set the tone. Will it work? Donald S. Garrett, a vice president at the airline consulting firm of Sineat Helliesen and Eichner, offers some extremely cogent and prudent commentary on the commodity trap. "When your service goes down the tube, the marketplace learns about it right away. With improvement, the marketplace moves more slowly."[14]

There are a number of companies outside the banking industry that employ this value added approach, including companies like Orville Redenbacher, Famous Amos, Frank Perdue, Cross Pen, American Express, and Nordstroms. The managements of these companies understand the concept of value added and have incorporated it into their product/service offering. What about banks?

Traditionally, the banking industry has imported value from outside the industry. By offering customers a free umbrella, toaster, or blanket if they open a checking account, banks have attempted to add value to their products and services. Some banks still offer compact discs, computers, and other more high tech items, but the situation is still the same. Banks are importing value from outside the industry and in so doing are implicitly admitting that there is nothing inherent in what they do as bankers that can add value to their offering. *This is wrong headed thinking!*

Customers value service. They value a bank that is accessible, that is responsive to their needs, a bank that does not make mistakes and when it does corrects those mistakes itself limiting the amount of hassle the customer has to go through.

Outstanding customer service can add value to the product or service offering of a bank. It can give bank management the freedom to avoid or escape the commodity trap, to charge higher prices, and to reduce long-term costs.

If one lesson can be learned from the banking wars, it is this: Customers are not as sensitive to price increases as once thought they would be. *If a higher price means greater perceived value, most bank customers will not desert their relationship with their bank over a marginal increase in price!* There is greater pricing freedom than was originally thought as long as the price-value relationship remains in equilibrium. A *Wall Street Journal*/NBC News poll captures this sense of pricing insensitivity on the part of customers. When 1,507 customers were asked, "How often do you purchase from a business that has excellent service but higher prices?" 75% responded either "sometimes" (40%), "most of the time" (28%) or "all of the time" (7%).[15] Outstanding service can offset higher prices!

Outstanding customer service has the added benefit of turning your contented and satisfied customers into walking, talking billboards that extol the quality of your service and products. High levels of customer service make buyers out of your customers instead of sellers out of your employees. Outstanding customer service has the capacity to keep customers in your bank reducing the need to attract new customers.

Lesson 7: Customer Retention and Employee Retention Go Hand-in-Hand

One of the less trumpeted, yet important aspects of top notch customer delivery systems is the relationship between customer satisfaction and employee turnover. Projections of qualified service personnel for the upcoming decade signal problems for many personnel managers throughout the service sector making employee retention a critical issue. Inconsistency in the employee ranks can mean inconsistency in the levels of customer service that an organization offers. Just what is this relationship between employee retention and solid customer service and how does it work?

Leonard A. Schlesinger and James L. Heskett offer the following depiction of the relationship shown in Figure 1-1. As the figure suggests, this is a cyclical relationship. It is difficult to say where the cycle begins and where it ends, but the point is clear. Satisfied customers mean low customer turnover which leads to higher profit margins. Higher profit margins in turn lead to greater employee satisfaction and less employee turnover and result in greater customer satisfaction. Delta Airlines is a good example of the employee-customer linkage. Delta's workers earn, on average, 21% more than the average airline worker. Good morale and a record of no layoffs over the past 33 years have contributed to an employee loyalty that has earned Delta the fewest number of customer complaints (of major carriers) for the past 16 years.[16]

Employees that are trained and empowered to give good service tend to take a greater pride in their work than those who are not equipped to deal with customers. One hospital that has embraced a customer service focus has as its basic strategy statement, "Proud to serve because we care." Its entire service strategy pivots on three basic values, "pride," "service," and "caring," three values that are easily and readily transferred to a bank setting.

Figure 1–1
The Service Cycle

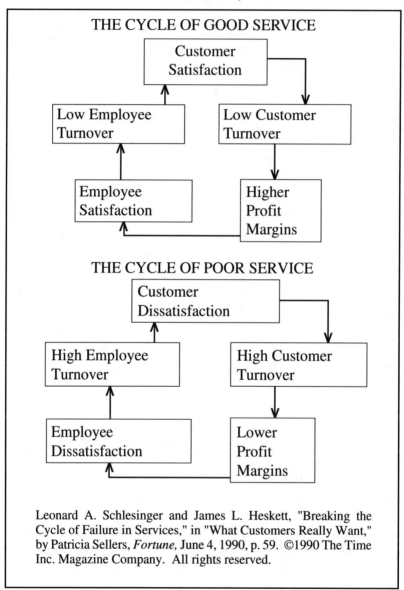

These are some of the basic lessons that we have learned from banks and other companies trying to compete in a service arena. But, perhaps the most important lesson that customer service driven organizations have learned is the importance of listening to their customers. Instead of developing notions of what outstanding service is in the vacuum of the boardroom, outstanding service deliverers have invested heavily in listening to what their customers say outstanding service is. Because this customer driven concept of service is so critical to the success of these top service organizations, we want to revisit some of the key points customers told us about what top notch service means to them. The next chapter explains how we were able to explore this important topic. Chapters 3, 4, and 5 allow the reader to listen in on the conversations about customer service as told to us by banking customers across the country.

Endnotes

1. Amanda Bennett. "Many Consumers Expect Better Service—And Say They Are Willing to Pay for It," *Wall Street Journal*, November 12, 1990, p. B1.
2. Amanda Bennett. "Making the Grade with the Customer," *Wall Street Journal*, November 12, 1990, p. B8.
3. William A. Davidson and Bro Uttal. "Coming: The Customer Service Decade," *Across the Board*, November 1989, p. 35.
4. Ibid.
5. Luke S. Helmes. "Seafirst Bank's Service Strategy," *The Channel*, Winter 1990, p. 4.
6. Davidson and Uttal, p. 35.
7. Ibid, p. 35.
8. Stephen Phillips, Amy Dunkins, James B. Treece and Keith H. Hammonds. "King Customer," *Business Week*, March 12, 1990, p. 88.
9. Ibid, p. 88.
10. Ibid, p. 88.
11. Seth Lubove. "Full Speed Ahead—but Cautiously," *Forbes*, October 29, 1990, p. 37.

12. Phillips *et. al.*, p. 88.

13. Ibid, p. 88.

14. Bridget O'Brian. "Continental Air's Coddling of Customers Pivotal to its Image Upgrade in Overhaul," *Wall Street Journal*, December 5, 1990, p. A11.

15. Amanda Bennett, p. B1.

16. Lubove, p. 37.

Chapter

Listening to Your Customers

The primary question that we sought to address from a research point of view was, "What do customers say quality of service in banking means to them?" The current answer to this question, in our opinion, is somewhat ambiguous.

The lack of a clear answer does not come from the lack of opinions among bankers about service. On the contrary, bankers tend to have well-defined opinions of what customers want with respect to quality of service. However, our experience and research suggest that these opinions, in many cases, have been influenced over the years by what banks can comfortably deliver and not what customers want or need. *In other words, we feel that bankers' definitions of quality have been developed with an inward bank focus rather than an outward customer focus.*

This can be illustrated by the following example. We have talked with numerous bankers who have told us that accuracy with transactions is the most important component in establishing a quality-of-service experience with customers. However, this is not how customers see it. Customers, by contrast, tell us that accuracy, 100-percent accuracy, is *expected*. The presence of accuracy does not provide customers with the *perception* of good service, but its absence definitely creates the perception of poor quality. In our opinion, the best that 100-percent accuracy can cause is a neutral perception by customers. Any bank that builds a quality-of-service program around accuracy is missing the point and will not be successful in creating positive perceptions among its customers. This kind of difference in perceptions is the reason bankers must look to customers for quality-of-service direction and definition.

In addition to a rather ill-defined definition of service quality, other characteristics of the research question are relevant. For example, we did not begin our research by presupposing that we knew what customers wanted. We took care not to define the research problem too narrowly. Our opinions are no better than those of bankers in this regard, one reason being that we are, by employment history, bankers. The focus of research had to be sufficiently broad to allow customers nearly free rein to explore for themselves what quality of service in banking means. Service quality exists, to a very large extent, in the world of perceptions.

Finally, we felt the need to provide a forum for consumer voices in the research setting. We sought to develop this book primarily around what customers told us, not around our empirical distillation of what they said by way of response to a self-limiting questionnaire. We wanted to allow the minds of customers to wander, restrained only by their experiences and expectations of banking relationships. To do that, we developed the sample discussion guide shown in Figure 2-1.

Nation-Wide Focus Groups

With the definition that we gave to the research problem, we chose to utilize a series of focus groups. This allowed us to lend customer definition to the concept of service quality, allowed the customers to define the specific direction of the research, and allowed them substantial amounts of freedom to explore their perceptions, attitudes, values, and expectations—all of which play a part in defining quality-of-service experiences.

Figure 2-1
Sample Discussion Guide

I.   Introduction

II. When you think of good quality of service in banking, what is the first thing that comes to mind?

III. When you think of bad quality of service in banking, what is the first thing that comes to mind?

IV. Tell the single most positive banking experience you have ever had.

V.   Tell the single most negative banking experience you have ever had. Was there anything that could have been done to handle the situation better? What would you have liked to see happen to turn this into a positive banking experience?

VI. Equate going to the bank with one of your routine daily activities.

VII. Discussion leader will explain the *Marketing Concept*. The Marketing Concept states that everything an organization does is done with customer satisfaction in mind. Is the Marketing Concept practiced in your bank? What is your opinion?

VIII. How does your bank perform on the following issues, and how important is each to you?

- Decision-making
- Consistency
- Promptness
- Personal service
- Being first
- Professionalism

- Accuracy
- Knowledge
- Price/value
- Performance
- Product features
- Reliability

Figure 2-1 *continued*

- Communication   • Dispute resolution
- Stability   • Courtesy

IX.   How long are you willing to wait for a teller? An account service representative? A banker or loan officer? What is acceptable? How long must a wait be before you get mad?

X.   How does the physical appearance of the banking facility affect your perception of the quality of service provided?

XI.   Are all banks basically alike? What distinguishes them? Which bank is "best" and why?

XII.   If you were looking for a new bank, what would you look for? Whom would you ask? How do you decide? Where do you go for information?

XIII.   What determines a "friendly" bank? Is being "friendly" important? What else is important?

XIV.   If a bank promises "superior service" what does this mean to you? Do you expect the bank to be perfect? If a bank does make a mistake, does this necessarily mean poor quality of service?

XV.   Thank the participants.

Next, we decided to conduct focus groups in various markets. Our purpose was to develop an understanding of service that transcends market boundaries. We sought to have representation via focus groups in each major geographic area of the United States. We conducted group interviews from the West Coast to the East Coast and from the Northeast to the South. Specific markets were chosen in the different geographic areas. The responses we received were shaped by the following factors: (1) individual bank willingness to sponsor focus groups and give us access to their customers; (2) bank willingness to assist in underwriting the expenses associated with the interviews; and (3) bank willingness to permit the use of the interview content in this book. Given these factors, the responses tend, if anything, to paint a picture of customer perceptions of banks that are already at least somewhat customer oriented. This technique enabled us to attain our goal: giving customers a voice toward defining the true meaning of quality of customer service.

Numerous banks across the country were contacted to determine their interest in quality of service from the customer's perspective. We found that many bankers were not interested in sponsoring focus groups with their customers. This was unexpected. We had felt that, because the focus groups constituted free consultation, our problem would be in excluding interested banks. Even so, many banks did respond enthusiastically the first time we approached them. So, the choice of banks was not random, but research was conducted only in markets that had a bank interested in quality of customer service.

The banks that agreed to sponsor focus groups generated tangible benefits. For example, several of them video taped the sessions where customers were talking about experiences that made them feel they had received good service. After video taping two to four hours of focus group interviews, these banks edited the tapes and constructed training tapes for their employees. We can think of no more powerful training tool than having customers tell employees directly what their quality-of-service expectations are.

Many banks also invited members of senior management to view the conduct of the focus groups. It seems that senior management can become rather far removed from customer service issues. Senior management has other, corporate-level issues on which it rightfully spends its time. However, we feel that there is no more important long-term issue for senior management than quality of service. This research allowed bankers who were closer to customers on a daily basis to make some critical points with senior management without putting their careers on the line to do it. Customers did it for them.

The research was a powerful tool for communicating up the hierarchy the importance of service quality. It also helped some banks make resource allocation decisions in favor of addressing customer concerns. One bank told us of rejecting the development of an advertising campaign recommended by its ad agency; the decision was based on input obtained from the focus groups. The bank became convinced, after listening to its customers, that the new advertising direction was inappropriate and should be studied and redirected. Another bank told us of a major promotional campaign that was scrapped pending further communication with its customers about their needs and wants.

Thus real, tangible benefits were gained immediately by banks willing to undertake this type of research project, in addition to the benefit of developing service quality definitions from the customer's perspective.

Initial Results of the Focus Group Analysis

Significant time was spent in background research on the quality issue. Much has been written that is useful. Of particular value to our efforts is the work of three researchers from Texas A&M: A. Parasuraneum, Valarie A. Zeithamel and Leonard L. Berry. Their article, "A Conceptual Model of Service Quality and its Implications for Future Research," formed the basis for our book. In it they identified 10 determinants of service quality that are applicable to many service industries. It was our intention to build on their initial work and to relate those 10 determinants to the banking industry in a manner bank managers are able to understand.

The following list includes determinants of quality identified by Parasuraneum, Zeithamel and Berry, along with some initial explanation of their meaning. Immediately following this list is an explanation of service quality that is used throughout the remainder of this book and on which our analysis of quality determinants is based.

1. *Reliability.* Customers want a bank and a banker that are reliable. That is, they want to do business with bankers who treat them the same no matter what changes occur in bank policy. They want bankers to be accurate, consistent, dependable, know their job, and do it correctly the first time; and they want the bank to do what it says it will do. Reliability means consistency, dependability, following through, and respect. It produces perceptions of security.

2. *Responsiveness.* Customers want bank personnel to display the willingness and readiness to provide service, to call the customers quickly in the event of an inquiry, to answer questions quickly and correctly, and to help the customers stay informed about their business. Customers want banks to process transactions quickly and also answer the telephone quickly. Responsiveness means sensitivity to needs, flexibility, going the extra mile, personal focus, willingness to follow up, and solving problems.

3. *Competent.* Customers want bankers to possess the necessary skills to do their jobs and to be knowledgeable and skillful contact personnel, support personnel, and management. Bankers must know how each product works. Competence means knowing your job, being accurate, having bank systems that work, and giving answers not guesses.

4. *Accessibility.* Customers want bankers with whom they can get in touch by phone or in person in a timely manner. They want banks to be open during hours that are convenient to the markets being served. Customers do not want excessive waits. They expect every teller station to be staffed during busy times of the day. Accessibility means being approachable and being available.

5. *Courtesy.* Customers want bank personnel to be polite, show respect, be considerate and friendly, neat in appearance, and demonstrate a sincere willingness to help. Customers do not want insincerity, and they can spot it easily. Courtesy means friendliness, consideration, and respect for the individual.

6. *Credibility.* Customers want a bank that is trustworthy, believable, and honest. They are more sophisticated about their banking relationships than bank advertisers give them credit for in their promotions. Credibility means believability and the effect of reputation, longevity, and physical appearance of the staff and facility.

7. *Understanding.* Customers want a banker who will learn from them what their specific requirements are, provide individual attention, and recognize them. Understanding means learning the individual's specific needs, giving personal attention, involvement, and recognizing regular customers.

8. *Communication.* Customers want banks to keep them informed in a way that they can understand. They want bankers to explain products and services—their costs and trade-offs between level of service and cost. They want assurance that their problems will be handled promptly and correctly and that personnel are well informed enough to explain a service or product, not merely repeat a printed message on a brochure. Communicating means keeping customers informed, initiating communications, and using customer language.

Now that we have identified the initial dimensions of customer service quality, several issues deserve mention. First, quality of service is a multidimensional concept and thereby very complex. It means different things to different people. Also, the relative importance of the dimensions changes with different customer groups. Second, what is important to customers may be quite different from what is important to a bank's management team. The importance of the dimensions cannot be assessed for a given bank without talking to its customers. Third, do not minimize the value customers place on service. The personal side of banking may make or break a quality experience. Fourth, these dimensions of quality of service are all interrelated. They should be considered as a whole rather than as distinct components. Fifth, there is a relativity to quality of service. A quality experience is related to the customer's expectations. Sixth, quality of service changes. What is a quality experience today may turn sour tomorrow unless managed astutely.

Model of Quality Service

From the above identification of the dimensions of customer service quality, we offer the model depicted in Figure 2-2. The model represents our distillation of information that we heard customers give their bankers.

We believe that reliability, competence, credibility, security, and physical appearance all combine to produce professionalism on the part of banks and bankers. This is the technical part of the model that yields a definition of who and what the bank is. Responsiveness, courtesy, and accessibility combine to form the interpersonal part of the model. This is how banks *approach* their customers. Finally, we feel understanding and communication combine to form what we call *knowing* the customer. This is where banks reach a common mind with consumers and bases quality of service on the definition given by their customers.

Professionalism, interpersonal relationships, and knowing customers all have expectation-versus-performance issues with which banks must deal. Customers have rather definite expectations relative to reliability, accuracy, accessibility, communication, and the other aspects of service that influence what level of performance is required to establish a perception of high quality. It is more complicated than combining quality dimensions, because customers bring expectations to the quality equation. For

Figure 2-2
The Customer Service Quality Model

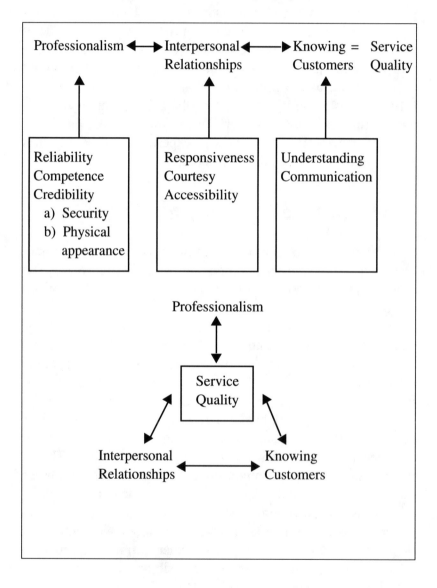

example, a bank may be the most responsive in the country, but if its advertising effort has created expectations in the minds of customers that exceed its actual performance, then customers will not experience outstanding service. We will deal with this in more detail in subsequent chapters.

Note that, in the model of quality service, we have connected professionalism, interpersonal relationships, and knowing customers with arrows pointing in both directions. This displays the interrelatedness of all components of the model.

The next three chapters discuss the professionalism, interpersonal relationships, and knowing customer components of the quality model. Throughout these chapters you will note the liberal use of customer stories and experiences around which we chose to build this book.

Chapter

Professional Aspects of Service

As mentioned in the previous chapter, service quality is a complex concept. While there might be many different ways in which it can be represented, we view it as consisting of three dimensions. The dimension with which this chapter is concerned is what we call the professional dimension. Bank customers told us that there are three aspects to professionalism: competence, reliability, and credibility. Listen to what your customers mean by competent, reliable, and credible service!

Competence

Competence is a difficult term to define. In many respects, it is a term like *pornography,* which, when a judge was asked what it was he said, "I can't define it but I sure know it when I see it!" Bank customers have a fairly consistent view of what they mean when they talk about competent service. Following are some ways they describe competency or a lack of it after having seen it.

Competence Means Knowing Your Job

From a North Carolina customer:

> One problem I see is a very high level of total incompetency in the loan department. But they get so much paper work on you, you could weigh it by the pound. Often the loan people are paid very little, and they really are not very sophisticated in business matters. You are way ahead of them. They are just not capable of dealing with your needs. It is nice to deal with someone who knows exactly what they need from you, because you do not want to have to put your entire financial package together every time you need money. Often you have a guy who looks in his notebook—somebody who says a customer has to meet all 22 steps to get a loan. That type of procedure is just a pain in the neck!

In this same vein is the comment from a customer in Mississippi:

> I am a Certified Financial Planner and do consulting work for small banks. The other day a lady from a client bank came to me for help analyzing a complicated deal. She did not have a clue as to how to go through a basic corporate tax return on a staggered year end. I felt sorry for her.... Some basic training would really have helped her understand things.

And this from a customer in Nebraska:

> One element of competency is being able to make a decision. I have waited nine months to hear on a line of credit. If they do not want to give it to me, okay. Just tell me!

These people are all saying the same thing. To them competency means *knowing how to do your job*. Too often bank customers are confronted by bank employees who do not know how to do their basic jobs. Good-quality service depends on everyone in the bank knowing how to perform their jobs right the first time. This, in turn, results from good, solid training. And, while many banks are doing a good job training their people, it is not uncommon to find new employees placed in jobs for which they have not been trained adequately.

The one comment we heard from a banker who has done considerable work on service quality is that his biggest problem is simply one of competence. Giving people the skills to do their jobs is an *absolutely necessary* first step to becoming a top service deliverer.

Competence Means Accuracy

Perhaps the most important aspect of competence, in the opinions of customers, is the idea of accuracy.

Put yourself in the position of one young woman from California, who comments on the accuracy of her former bank:

> I was nine and a half months pregnant. We had moved out of our house, all our belongings were in a van, and we were waiting for our new house to close. The bank took our downpayment check of $830.00 and incorrectly posted it as $.83. Our downpayment did not clear. It was a court probate sale on the house, and when you have the court involved, well.... For three days we did not have a place to move to, with all we owned in the moving van. I went into the bank to try and get the check straightened out, and the girl said, "I cannot do anything about this; it will take several days to get straightened out." I was standing in the bank, nine and a half months pregnant, crying hysterically. It was hot and I had no place to move. My husband came in, went directly to the president, and got it straightened out. But it had taken three days just to see the president!

This same theme of accuracy was repeated over and over again. Here are two customers from Colorado and New York, respectively, talking about accuracy and their banks. These comments are typical of those that we heard nationwide:

> I expect my bank to be accurate to the penny, there should be no margin for error. They should be perfect, 100-percent accurate, especially with my money. But you cannot blame a whole bank for one teller's mistake. As long as the bank can correct the mistake, that is okay. When they say, "No, we cannot do anything for you," well, that is a different story.

A special aspect of the accuracy component of competence is conveyed in this comment by a man from Chicago:

> The main thing with any mistake, not just banking, is, once it is brought to someone's attention, what effort is made to correct it?

This is not what occurred with another customer. She relates a story about her former bank:

> I made a lump-sum payment on my principal, and the bank showed it all wrong. It was so fouled up I could not believe it. I tried to get it straightened out and talked to many people. They made me feel stupid, that it was all my fault. But they still could not get it right. Another statement came from the bank, and it was still wrong! How was I to report my interest to the IRS? This problem was never resolved. I have no confidence in my bank!

Several things can be learned from these customers' comments on accuracy. First and foremost is that customer expectations regarding bank accuracy are very high. Overall, bank customers appear to have a solid regard for the level of accuracy that their banks offer them. This is the good news. The bad news is that any deviation from this strong expectation runs the risk of sending a strong message of incompetence to the customers and a strong vote of "no confidence" in the service area.

Almost a paradox, however, is the willingness of customers to forgive an error if, as the gentleman from Chicago indicated, someone will do something about it. This suggests that, while error-free banking should be a goal of all bank managements, error correction should also be an extremely high management priority. Furthermore, customers are wise to the old dodge of computer errors. Many have computers in their homes. They understand that, when the computer makes a mistake, it does so because it is directed to do so by a human.

A second concern of many customers is the inability of banks to acknowledge their mistakes. Many customers seem to feel that their banks first attempt to convince them that errors are their fault. When it is pointed out that the errors result from bank mistakes, seldom if ever do the banks apologize for the errors or for blaming the customers. This has two negative effects. First, the original errors are frustrating for the customers. Second, the questioning of the customers' intelligence or competence hardens their negative feelings toward the banks.

Consequently the issue of error resolution becomes paramount. The goal is to rectify the mistake and *keep a satisfied customer.* The best advice that we can give for handling errors is: *Do not handle an error, handle a quality encounter!*

A final message that we gleaned from the conversations about competence has to do with the speed of error reconciliation. To customers, banks that corrected mistakes quickly generated stronger feelings of quality service than those that dragged the process on or forgot to do anything about it.

Giving customers access to management to redress a problem is a good idea. Too often they have to present their cases to tellers who do not know how to handle the situation. Typically the customers are told that they must see so and so, and of course so and so is never around. The customers then are told that they will have to come back. This is ridiculous. There is no reason that someone other than the mythical so and so who is never around cannot help them. Asking customers to come back only exacerbates a bad situation, one that you want handled quickly and effortlessly on your customers' part. The onus is on the bank to keep the customer. After all, customers have numerous other options, usually within walking distance.

Another option was exercised by a woman who moved from California to Philadelphia:

> I moved from Monterey, California, and brought a $300,000 cashiers check with me to Philadelphia. My husband was in the service. I went to XYZ Bank to set up my checking and savings accounts, explaining that I needed to write lots of big checks right away. They said, "Fine, no problem, it is a cashiers check." I went out the next day, found the house we wanted, and wrote a check for the downpayment. I went to a furniture store and bought enough furniture to fill a three-bedroom house, went to the grocery store, and got the kids into private

school. All of a sudden, five days later, I got notices from the bank telling me that all of my checks bounced! The bank had set up my checking account but given me checks with a different number. Every check bounced. My car insurance was cancelled by the insurance company. They would not even accept a letter from the bank. My house fell through. In five days I had lost everything! It took three lawyers to get everything straightened out. All I got from the bank was, "Gee, we are sorry. We make mistakes once in a while." Needless to say, I switched my account to another institution immediately.

Competence Means Systems That Work

A third component of competence, often overlooked, is the behind-the-scenes operations that are responsible for much of what customers receive in the mail. The quality of service many customers receive is, in their opinions, directly associated with the size of the institution:

> In a big bank . . . a mistake, whether a lost check, a deposit getting lost, etcetera, can take five months to get straightened out. It took me five months to get a misposting of a check straight at my bank. At my new bank I can sit down and get it fixed right then. There are so many behind-the-scenes people there who do a really great job. I do not want to have a bloodletting experience to get a bank error straightened out. That seems to be what happens in a big bank: *you* have the responsibility to straighten out a bank error.

We believe that, as merger and acquisition activity increases, so too will problems in service delivery. The concern is that banks are growing beyond their capabilities to service their increasing structures.

Consider the problem encountered by one of our fellow Mississippians, who attempted to cash a check drawn on the home office in a newly acquired branch in a different part of the state. He was told that the branch, even though it was part of the banking system, could not cash his check. He found this particularly irksome after having read the advertising for the bank, which boasted border-to-border service for its customers. Apparently, not all customers.

Competence Means Getting Answers, Not Guesses

One final aspect of competency is worth describing. This is from a customer in California:

> It is dealing with someone who really knows what he or she is doing and getting the service right. The branch I deal with has competent people, because every time I call I do not get a round-about answer to my questions. I do not ask a question only to be put on hold for a long period of time. If a person does not know an answer, they say they do not and that they will contact someone else and get back to me. And they do it. I think the fact that they do not know an answer is not an indication of incompetence. I would rather get the right answer than someone's wrong guess!

Summary—Competence

Customers told us that, for them to judge their bankers as competent, the bankers had to know their jobs. The bankers had to be accurate, have systems that work, and provide definitive answers rather than guesses. Bankers who do not provide all these elements are not viewed as competent and worthy of the customers' relationships.

Reliability

Just as there are four components of competence, customers define reliability, the second aspect of the technical dimension of quality, as having four components. These components are consistency, dependability, follow-through, and respect.

Reliability Means Consistency

When we asked bank customers to tell us what they meant when they said they want a reliable relationship with their banks, we continually heard comments such as the following from a small business owner in California:

> Consistency. I know what to expect every time I go in. The rules do not change because they made a bad loan in South

America. Let me explain why I say that. For many years I had an excellent relationship with the XYZ Bank. I went in one day to renew my company's credit and they said, "Our policy has changed on businesses of your size. In order to get a line of credit, you and your other officers will have to take out a personal loan that the bank will pool and use as your line of credit." Our credit record with the bank was incredibly good, yet they would not renew a business line of credit without personal loans. This new policy became effective, coincidentally, when the bank began to lose its fanny in South America. We transferred all of our money to another bank, which had no problem establishing our line of credit. The new bank bent over backwards to help us. They even called us and *dropped* our line of credit rate by 1/4 percent because of the balance we keep in our account.

Consistency leads to predictability, and everyone seeks predictable relationships. This is especially true when the relationship is with one's financial institution. Being a bank that customers can count on means that the bank must be willing to establish policies that it can honor consistently. Without this consistency, customers cannot count on the relationship, no matter how sound and how solid the bank is.

Reliability Means Dependability

Closely related to the idea of consistency is the idea of dependability. The difference, we would speculate, hinges on the idea of your customers trusting the relationship in a more personal manner. Dependability, to many banking customers, means that their bank will not violate the bond of faith that exists between customer and institution. Here, in the words of a furrier from California, is a good example of what dependability means to many bank customers:

My bank had okayed a charge of $3,000.00 at my store, even though I told them I thought the Mastercard was bad. Three months later they came back to me, saying that the card was bad! I felt it was pretty cut and dried, but no one would talk to me at the bank. They debited my account for the $3,000.00

even though they had authorized the charge! Finally I had to call my lawyer. They talked to him and eventually paid the $3,000.00, but I felt *betrayed*. A bank that had helped me so much in the past—all of a sudden I was not "big enough." When they were small and I was small, it was fine. They grew faster than I did and would not communicate with me. They even treated me like I had done something wrong!

In listening to this customer's story, one gets the distinct impression that he had established a relationship with the bank that exceeded a normal business relationship. His sense of betrayal is more like the denial of a friendship by one of his friends because he does not value the other person as he once did. The bond of dependability was broken, as was the relationship between bank and customer.

Here is another perspective on dependability, not too unlike the previous one. This is from a customer in Nebraska:

> Back East, where we used to bank, a really bad thing happened. I got my paycheck, took it to the bank, deposited it, and got my receipt. Somewhere in the process, the check was "eaten." It was shredded. The bank proceeded to debit my account and bounced all of my checks, this despite the fact that I had more than enough in savings to cover the checks. We had been banking there a number of years. When I gave them the check, it was whole and in one piece. I had a deposit slip! To me that was a nightmare. I had not done anything incorrectly. They had ruined it and then proceeded to bounce my checks even though it was their error. And they did not even call me or check my other accounts. That day we took our money out and went elsewhere.

Finally, consider this customer's relationship with his bank:

> The bank that we were previously with made a statement to the press as to what would happen if there were to be a recession and how they were responding to protect themselves. The bank said that they were reassessing their relationships with clients who might be impacted by a recession.... Being in

the retail construction business and knowing the retail trade would be hit hard by a recession, (I knew they were) telling me, "We are not interested in your business, because we are afraid there might be a recession." I took that as the old attitude, "There's nothing to fear but fear itself." After reading that article, I had never felt so infuriated and so betrayed!

There appears to be an implicit linkage between customers and their banks that the customers recognize more strongly than do the banks. The sense of rejection and anger customers feel when their banks fail to react in a dependable manner is strong and real. Customers want to feel as though their banks are friends, not just institutions. They want to trust these friends, and when that trust is not returned there is a strong sense of rejection. This may be one of the most important aspects of the service relationship between bank and customer. Abrogation of the dependability factor may be more damaging to the relationship than any other action.

Reliability Means Following Through

Few moments in the relationship between a bank and its customers are more frustrating than those in which the bank has said, "Do not worry; we will take care of it for you," and then nothing is done. Reliability means that, when a banker says something will be done, it gets done and gets done right. Here is a story from a California man about follow-through. In his story you will also discover several other ways to destroy a potential customer relationship through poor service.

> I had been approached several times by the XYZ Bank saying that they wanted me as a customer and could give me a higher line of credit than I had at my present bank. This would sure make my life easier. I decided to go with the XYZ Bank. Everything I had done at my other bank I had essentially done on a handshake and then later signed the papers and concluded the deal. I thought this was the way it was done everywhere. As mentioned the XYZ Bank promised a greater line of credit than I had at my former bank. Six months after I had moved

everything there, I got a very curt couple of lines of typing on a form (that did not even look like the right form) saying I had been denied the line of credit! I called and learned the woman who had approached me had left. I phoned several times to talk with someone about this, and none of my calls were ever returned. Finally I reached the branch manager, who hemmed and hawed and said he would look into it. I explained I was going to New York on a buying trip in a few days and needed to know something. He never called me, nor were there any messages on my return. So, I went to see the vice president above the manager. He knew nothing of my problem, even after I called to schedule a meeting. I said, "It sounds to me like you really do not need me in your bank." He said, "You're right."

Failure to follow through on a customer's request or business leads to a number of problems. First, the banker demonstrates a definite lack of competence. Instead of solving problems, the banker creates additional problems—and these problems are usually thrown back on the customer. Perhaps more important, as we will soon discuss, the banker creates a problem of credibility that will haunt most future transactions with the customer if he or she stays with the bank.

Reliability Means Respect

The final component of the reliability dimension that customers identified was good old-fashioned respect:

> To me dependability means respect. They treat businesses with respect because they realize you are at risk and so are they. I see them treating business people as if they really do matter! My bank does this better than any bank I have ever dealt with.

In this idea of respect is the notion of valuing the customer. This involves knowing that the customer could bank at a number of different banks. In this case, the customer chose your bank. This is a valuable relationship and one that should be valued as such.

In the following statement, a customer expresses the idea of respect somewhat differently, but the meaning is still clear:

> I think I will always have an account at my bank. When I first came to this city, I was even poorer than I am now—five kids at home, mortgages on everything, and I worked for a company that went under. For several weeks I would deposit my checks on Friday. I would write checks all weekend to pay my bills. Monday, Tuesday, and Wednesday all my checks would come back . . . bounced! On Tuesday or Wednesday my paycheck would come back. It had bounced too! I would take my paycheck to my company, and they would make it good in cash. Then I would take the cash to the bank. It had honored all the checks that I had written on Monday, Tuesday, and Wednesday. Not once was one *not* paid. I do not know who at my bank cared about me, but somebody did. This was 30 years ago, and I did not have overdraft protection. I will always have a warm spot in my heart for my bank.

How many of your customers would say that about their relationship with your bank? Mutual respect—respect by the customer for the reliability of service the bank provides and respect on the part of the bank for the customer—is the basis for a strong and lasting relationship. Where does this respect and value for the customer come from? Where just about everything else comes from in the bank, at least according to a customer from Chicago:

> Attitude of the management. A lot of small banks that started around here have the same approach—they are going to be service oriented. I used to be with one bank, but when they were bought out that attitude began to change. Finally the sense of familiarity and respect was lost. I felt like the guy who was asked to dance and then left in the middle of the dance floor!

Need we say more?

Reliability Produces Security

The last component of reliability is security. Bank customers who feel their banks are reliable also tend to feel that their relationships are secure. By security, we do not mean the financial solvency of the bank. This is essentially taken for granted by most bank customers.

Instead, bank customers tend to think of security as a warm, fuzzy feeling not too distant from the idea of dependability. Here, let some customers tell you:

> My bank protected me real well one time. I was in a hurry and I wrote a check. My name was illegible. It was a pretty good-sized chunk of money. When the guy came in to cash it, my bank would not accept it because of my signature. They called me up and would not even take my okay over the phone. I had to go down there and write the man another check. I felt the bank was really protecting my interests. I appreciated that.

Said another customer:

> I mail a lot of my deposits in, and I feel very secure just knowing that there is someone there to handle my money for me.

When we tried to pin down customers to define security as exactly as they could, we heard statements like this:

> I called a branch to help my mom with her CD, and I asked for the officer. I was told that there was no officer there. I thought, "What!" I have now in my mind that I am not going to like that branch because there is not even an officer there. There should be someone in charge all the time.

It is obvious that the idea of security means different things to different people. The bottom line is that security is a feeling customers get when they know that their money will be handled professionally. This is related directly to several other factors that we have already discussed. It echoes a point that we made earlier and that we will keep repeating: All of these dimensions of customer service are related. Knowing your job, consistency, dependability, and follow-through, for example, are all related to and contribute to customers' perception that they have secure relationships with their banks.

Summary—Reliability

Reliability means consistency, dependability, following through, respect, and security. Customers like having bankers who are the same today as they will be tomorrow; in other words, they value consistency of treatment. This means across branches and cities, not just within the same bank. Additionally, customers want a dependable banker who will follow through to see a problem resolved. Reliability also produces perceptions of security concerning the bank and its employees.

Credibility

Credibility, ostensibly, means *believability*. Customers tell us that there are three aspects to being a credible bank: your reputation, the perceived longevity of the bank and the bank's physical appearance.

Credibility Means Believability

Believability has a very strong impact on a bank's reputation. How credible a bank is depends on two aspects of its relationship with its customers. First is the level of expectations customers have with respect to the level and quality of the service provided. Second is the actual experience they have when they deal with the bank. Very simply stated, when their expectations of service exceed the bank's delivery of that service, they are not going to be satisfied. Then the bank's credibility and ultimately its reputation are in jeopardy.

Here is how many customers feel about the credibility of their banks:

> What does it mean to me when a bank advertises personal service? It is meaningless. I have never seen an ad say, "We do not give you personal service."

> Some banks advertise "Free Checking," but they are not really telling the truth.

When asked how they respond to advertisements claiming solid customer service, this is the response:

> I do not believe it because they all say that.

> I will bet that of all the ads in Sunday's paper for banks, only three might do what they say in their ads!

Customers are skeptical and becoming more sophisticated. Service strategies, contrary to the apparent conventional wisdom of many bank advertisers, do not run on promises. They run on promises delivered:

> We quit a bank because everything they promised was not true. We were always told the pluses of their bank, but not how long it took to have a check go through or about their accuracy. Whenever I would go to cash a check, the computers were down. They closed at 4:00 p.m. and I did not get off until 5:00 p.m. It was awful. I know more than the tellers. It was a joke to go in there and I closed the account when they could not cash my $5 check.

> I had been waiting for word on a site development loan, and it really seemed to be taking a long time for approval. I dismissed the bank's delay on the idea that they were real busy. It finally came down to the statement, "We're curtailing our home building activity." I called the chairman of the bank, explaining the runaround I had been getting. We had a meeting, and I was told, "There was nothing in writing on the loan. You just assumed we would make you the loan." The statement that seemed inappropriate was, "Don't you think it was rather naive of you to assume we would make you a loan?" I felt like I had just been lead down the path.

Here is a conversation about the same bank and the experiences of two customers in Colorado:

First customer. "Bankers, to me, are the poorest business people in the world." Second customer. "You got that right. They do not know how to promote. They only try to knock you through the door. Once you are through, you never hear from them again. A good example is, I just left one bank to go to another. When someone moves $50,000 out of a bank, gosh, wouldn't you think they would call and ask why?" First customer. "Yeah, we went with that bank when they first opened. They were a small bank, made promises—'We will do this, we will do that.' Well, they did not, nor could they deliver what they promised."

One institution advertised lowest interest rates. But, as it turned out, once he started hitting that computer and telling me it will be 1/2 percent extra for this or that, the interest rate was what the competitor was offering. I viewed the ad as deceptive advertising. I have not gone back there because of that.

Finally, this about expectations and actualities from an upstate New Yorker.

You can use all those good-meaning words that everyone wants to hear. *But*, until you go and check it out, it does not mean two hoots and a holler!

That is a skeptical customer, but one who offers good advice.

Reputation and Longevity Affect Credibility

Well then, how do you tell whether a bank is believable or not? How do you tell if it gives good service or is simply making a lot of promises that it cannot keep? Customers tell us they use two basic cues to determine how credible a bank is:

If you want a bank that gives good service in this town, you simply have to ask anyone. They all know who does a good job and who does not.

You get a reputation for doing things well. Like, if you ask at the university where to go for student loans, they tell you real quick—XYZ Bank.

> You have to remember that it is people who make up the bank. The people at my bank are real personal and good with business people. They are not offensive. That is not true for the bank across the street, and everyone knows it. The bank across the street has a bad reputation, and it is hurting them!

There is little doubt that reputation is strategic money in the bank. As we pointed out in Chapter 1, dissatisfied customers talk and spread the word. This negative publicity is very powerful. It is significantly more credible than a bank's advertising efforts, because it is not controlled by the bank. A good reputation that is communicated by customers is probably worth most of a bank's advertising budget. Unfortunately, banks create many of their own problems in this regard. Raising expectations to unrealistic heights and then not being able to satisfy them only creates a credibility problem that is magnified by disgruntled customers.

The other cue that customers use is longevity. Unfortunately, this is out of the hands of many banks to create. It is more of a dividend that well-run, customer-oriented and service-conscious banks reap over an extended period of time. Here is what one New York customer told us about her impressions of a bank's longevity. This is typical of the responses we heard:

> Whenever I go into my bank, I see a lot of old people in there doing business. That is where they have their money. I look at my bank as, "This is old New York, this is the roots of New York." This has been my bank's image, and their reputation is built upon it. They exude a sense of permanence and confidence. This image is even more important today, with all the S&Ls that are failing.

Physical Appearance and Credibility

Although we have been told never to judge a book by its cover, in reality, physical appearance is a strong cue. Physical appearance of the bank sends a strong initial statement to customers about what kind of treatment they can expect. This can be a double-edged sword in some cases. Depending on specific markets, some customers will react negatively to a too-lavish bank decor, while others expect it.

Typical of customer comments against lavish interiors is this by a customer in California:

> It was a rather *plush* establishment. It felt rather snooty. I moved my account to a place that was not quite so plush. My bank does not need to spend that kind of money on surroundings.

The best advice appears to be to fit the physical appearance of the bank to the types of people you want to attract as customers. Bank appearance does not have to be lavish and expensive to make a statement of security, competence, and reliability.

Some customers tell us that they are sensitive to nonphysical aspects of the bank. One customer, who was typical of those indicating a sensitivity for more than the physical, said she was aware of what she called "vibrations":

> When I walk into a place, I get vibrations. I feel things. The people cause these vibrations. I want a place (and people) to do what I need to have done and not to look like it has millions of dollars. In my conscious mind, I am looking for a place that fits me.

Whether or not you believe in vibrations, this customer has just said something very important about service quality. Her bank "fits" her. This fit is a function not only of the physical setting, but of the people in the bank. Her bank fits her because it is there to serve her, and she knows it.

Summary—Credibility

For bankers to be considered credible, they must be believable, have good reputations, and enjoy longevity in the community. The bank must also have an appropriate physical appearance. Customers told us that they can sense the quality of service in the bank just by walking into the lobby. The physical appearance of the bank and the expectation the customer brings to the bank due to its community reputation all affect credibility. It is important to customer relationships to establish that you are believable and that customers can place faith in what you say and do.

Summary

This chapter has focused on one dimension of service quality, the professional dimension. We call it the professional dimension because the components that make it up—competence, reliability, and credibility—reflect a certain management dedication to doing the job right the first time, doing it on time, and creating an accurate and deliverable level of service quality. Like the other dimensions, this dimension is complex.

In many respects we got the impression that this is perhaps the most important aspect of service quality. Bankers also have told us that it represents one of the biggest challenges in attempting to become high-quality service deliverers.

Chapter

How Interpersonal Relationships Affect Service Quality

As the second part of the model of service quality described in Chapter 2, the interpersonal relationship dimension is concerned primarily with how the bank approaches customers in day-to-day interactions. Interpersonal relationships are the means by which banks convey professionalism (Chapter 3) to customers. The interpersonal relationship dimension consists of three basic components: responsiveness, courtesy, and accessibility. This chapter focuses on situations where responsive, courteous, and accessible behaviors serve to link professionalism and relationships to perceptions of service quality. Here's what your customers mean when they talk about responsiveness, courtesy, and accessibility.

Responsiveness

The first component of the interpersonal relationship dimension is responsiveness. The central issue here is that of meeting individual needs on time and efficiently.

Responsiveness Means
Being Sensitive to Needs

Responsiveness itself tends to be a complex quality issue with varying subcomponents. For example, to many customers, responsiveness means being sensitive to their needs. Consider the following comments from typical bank customers.

A customer from California said:

> I was applying recently for a real estate loan for a new house I am building. The loan officer said to me that the bank was a bit concerned about my occupation, real estate broker, since there has been a downturn in the real estate market. I reminded him that on the back of each loan application is the phrase, "We do not discriminate based on race, creed, color, etcetera." I asked, "What about occupation? It seems you are telling me that you do not want to loan me money because I am a real estate broker. That does not make sense." They went ahead and made me the loan. But that attitude seemed short-sighted. I got the impression the guy did not really understand real estate."

Even an innocent comment made by the banker started the customer questioning the bank's desire to continue the relationship. Just because the bank was concerned about real estate lending in general, there was no reason to be insensitive to this particular customer.

A man from North Carolina said:

> My son is over 18, and he goes through money as fast as he makes it. He cannot have a savings account unless he has a minimum of $250. Now that is ridiculous. They make it hard to encourage someone to save. That is a service they have cut out. Sure it costs the bank to maintain a $10-balance in savings, but that is not encouraging to a five-year old to have to acquire $250. Same thing about loans. I wanted to establish credit with a $1,000 loan. They would not loan me "as little" as $1,000.

Another customer from Colorado told of this situation:

> I own a daycare business, and consequently I have a lot of checks. My bank has told me that I should ask my customers for cash because, if I deposited checks, I could not write checks on my account right away. I went home in tears. I thought, "This is a joke." I did not want to tell all my customers that I had to have cash from them. I quit that bank right away.

This was evidence of insensitivity toward this businesswoman and her business.

And finally, one customer from Mississippi said:

> Banks should plan for lunch hour traffic and payday traffic. They should put more tellers out. Haven't they figured out their rush periods by now?

Apparently, this continues to be a troublesome issue for banks nationwide. Customers do not accept the logic of less-than-fully-staffed teller windows during high-traffic times. Many customers expressed concern that their banks were more sensitive to their tellers than to their customers.

Responsiveness Means Flexibility

Another subcomponent of responsiveness is flexibility. This concerns how well the bank can adapt to the changing needs of individual customers and how willing bank personnel are to make these changes. Consider the following comment from a woman in North Carolina:

> I needed a loan and went to where I had done my business for a number of years. They quoted me a rate, and I explained that I could get a better one elsewhere. I asked, "Do you want to work with me?" They said that was a firm rate and that, if I could get a better rate elsewhere, I had better go somewhere

else. I found out that bankers do not really care if you have been with them 20 years. You would think they would care, especially at the alarming rate of bank closings.... The problem here is that the bank was not flexible. Let's face it! In today's marketplace everybody knows you can negotiate for anything, and you ought to be able to negotiate the cost of funds depending on your credit and total relationship. I think that if banks had a more flexible pricing policy, they could satisfy the good customer and then explain why some people have to pay a higher rate.

Also, a customer from Nebraska said:

I had a CD at the bank I used and knew what rate (higher) I could get at another bank. I asked my bank if we could negotiate a rate and they would not, so they lost all my money. That's so sad. The bank is a service institution, or so they said. Why aren't they interested in service?

These customers knew that banks could or should negotiate rates to retain customers, especially after a 20-year relationship. However, the bank personnel in this situation were pricing from a typed rate sheet or menu that disregarded individual customer relationships. This was viewed as an overly inflexible bank policy. A woman from Florida gave the following example of flexibility:

I handle my elderly parents' finances. One CD of theirs was to mature in December, and I planned to transfer it to their checking account for them to live on. My husband became ill in December, and I forgot to withdraw the CD. I did not recall ever receiving a notice of maturity. After December I realized I had let the CD slip, and I called the bank to explain. They listened and responded by giving me the CD without penalty.

Rules did not govern the bank's relationship with this customer. The needs of the individual did.

Another customer, from New York, gave this example:

> When I began looking for a bank, I went to one where I knew some of the upper-level managers. I called them and explained my situation. They said they had a special program for people like me, called the Private Banking Program. I put together a financial statement and program showing what I wanted: a line of credit, qualification on long-term loans, mortgage help, venture capital. I explained that I just wanted to qualify for (these things) and wanted to know what the spread would be. They took a look and said, "Sorry, we cannot help you." It was not that the bank saw me as not creditworthy. Rather, it was just that I did not fit their policy profile, and they would make no exceptions. A second bank looked at me and was less concerned at fitting a policy profile.

Here, as in many examples we heard, the bank responded to customers from the perspective of rather fixed, rigid policies instead of individualized, flexible policies designed to address their needs.

Another interesting comment on flexibility came from a customer from California:

> Tellers shouldn't violate bank policy. I think that officers should be flexible, though. I think in this day banks have to start looking at those who have been loyal to them and give something back. I have learned not to have loyalty. I go where I get the best rates.

And from a customer from Washington:

> I don't think tellers should have the liberty to violate bank policy for me. But they should have immediate access to someone who can. How the teller handles this situation is very important. The teller should explain that the situation is understood, but he or she cannot make the decision. The teller must go to a manager, but I expect the manager to violate policy to serve my individual needs so long as it does not harm anyone.

The expectation from customers is not to have a totally flexible banking system. They understand the need for rules. But they want access to someone who can "bend" the rules when it is necessary in order to serve them.

And finally a customer from California relayed this story to us:

> I really like the fact that I can call my bank and transfer funds from one account to another. They will give me a reference to transaction number for that transfer and then, when I get my statement, I can check against that reference number. This is great, because I do not have to go down and sign anything. It is wonderful.

Responsiveness Means Going the Extra Mile

Another subcomponent of responsiveness is what we refer to as "going the extra mile." Consider the following examples from two customers in California:

> The first time we saw them walk into our office with our statement for the month, we almost fell over backwards. Hand-delivered statements! I also use their courier service, where they come by and pick up our deposit. How does that work? They come out at a time I determine best suits my business, sometimes mornings and sometimes afternoons. I can go for weeks without going into the bank.

> Another example of responsiveness: My company developed a form that allows us to transfer money from a hundred different accounts and pool the funds into one account.

> The bank worked with us so we wouldn't have to work up individual deposit and withdrawal slips. They were willing to accept our forms.

This was seen by the customers as something not required of the bank. It certainly was not *expected.* However, it told the customers something about their bank's willingness to deal with them individually.

Another example from a New York customer is:

> There was a period of time when the computer checks we had printed did not read in my bank's magnetic machines. It was a nightmare for awhile. My bank, however, had our checks

reprinted themselves. They were very accommodating in making sure the checks were compatible with our software and that we liked their looks. I thought the bank really went one step beyond.

The customer's final comment, "I thought the bank really went one step beyond," describes our going-the-extra-mile component of responsiveness.

And finally a customer from Texas told of this situation.

I have even called my bank at 6 p.m. at night and found people answering the phones. My business goes on at all hours, and I may have a question that does not come up between 9:30 and 3:00. In fact, they (questions) seem always to come up at 3:15! My bank is always there when I have a question and need an answer.

The bank kept people on the phones after hours to respond to customer inquiries. Again, this was viewed as an example of going the extra mile.

Responsiveness Means Having a Personal Focus

Perhaps the most important subcomponent of responsiveness is what we call personal focus. We say "perhaps the most important" because, in our focus groups, more examples were given of personal focus than any other subcomponent of responsiveness. When customers thought of responsiveness, they thought more often of the bank establishing the personal service bond with them. Here are several examples of establishing a personal focus. A customer from North Carolina said:

I went in to roll over a CD that had matured. The (woman) told me about three or four options. She didn't just take my money and write up the first thing we talked about. She gave choices. I wound up getting a better deal and I liked that. I too like to go into a bank and see a familiar face.

A Mississippi customer said:

When my wife went to deposit money into her savings account, the teller commented on the amount of money in the account and suggested she look into another type of investment where she might earn more interest. We thought it was great for that teller to bring this to our attention. I appreciate my banker making suggestions on investments.

A customer from Illinois told of this situation:

Why does big seem to denote lack of quality? I really don't know why size has anything to do with quality of service. I grew up in the Northwest when a department store was very small. My mom took me to the department store as a child to buy shoes. That store is just as good now as they were then, and they're huge and getting bigger in spite of the fact they are expensive. It is not cheap to do business with my bank, but I do not give a care about that. When I want something done, it is the convenience and ability to translate my idea to the bank and have them accept it and lend me the 100,000 bucks when (I) need it. You have got to be in a different league than I am in to get the personal attention from people like some bankers. But I get that personal attention from my bank, so I don't mind spending a little more.

The implication from this customer is that banks can demand a higher price for good-quality service.

And another customer from Colorado:

The reason I left my former bank was that I paid my property tax bill by mail. I had my deposit in my purse and was supposed to make it that day in addition to the thousand other errands I needed to do. Three or four days later, (I discovered) my deposit still in my purse! Meanwhile, the bank bounced my property tax check! Now that is a penalty. I called the bank and said, "After 20 years of my making regular deposits, why didn't you call me rather than bounce my property tax check?" The bank replied that it did not know who I was. It just puts these things in the computer, and when it shows O.D.... After 20 years they still don't know who I am.

Another example of personal focus comes from North Carolina:

Banks really *do not care* about the customer. I have been in management of a large corporation, and I find the people who are at the top do care. It is the people who work for them who don't have any concern as to whether they get your business or not. It is these people who go home at the end of the day and relax, and that is it. The next morning they drag up and say, "I gotta go back to that job again." I know the people at the top of a business care about customers.

And this example from a customer in Nebraska:

A good example of responsive service is this. I went to a store and wrote a check on my husband's account. I am authorized to sign on the account, but it only has his name on the checks. The clerk said, "You can't do this." I said, "Well, call the bank and talk to whomever answers the phone." He called and said that he had a check presented by a wife on her husband's account and wanted to make sure it was okay. And that was just whoever answered the phone, not the manager. The clerk hung up and said to me, "What do you do, own the bank?" It is wonderful to be made to feel you are someone special rather than a number.

And from two California customers:

One of the things I resented with my former bank was, after a 20-year banking relationship, I went to make a deposit, not a withdrawal, and it was over a certain amount. They had to get approval to accept my deposit. Come on now! I am giving them the money and I had to wait on an approval for a deposit. This makes no sense to me.

I am infamous for, when I sign the big stack of checks three times a week to all of our distributors, that I miss signing a check. Last week I failed to sign an employee's check. I don't care who calls my bank, she will say, "It is Susan's check, no problem. We will put it through." They will call me and, if they cannot reach me, they call my accountant to get an okay. I don't have to go down and sign it.

These comments indicate that, for a bank to be responsive to customers, it must develop a personal focus in its service delivery.

Responsiveness Is Willingness to Follow Up

Another subcomponent of responsiveness is the willingness of the bank to follow up with the customer. Consider the following example from Nebraska:

> I had to do a stop payment. The banker who helped me with it had initially made an error and said the check had not gone through, so she put a stop payment on it. Then, when I came in the next day, the check had gone through. I called about it and the banker who had helped me was friendly and helpful and said evidently something had gone wrong. She explained it and handled it and even called back the next day to tell me everything had gone okay. I really appreciated the followup. I was real surprised, because sometimes a customer can get lost in the shuffle. But she took the time to assure me, and I was real impressed.

Responsiveness also means getting back to customers on a timely basis, as evidenced by another customer from Nebraska:

> My checking account is such that I don't get my checks back in my statement, but the bank tells (me) that (I) can request a check if I need it. I asked for one back, and you know how long it took before I got it? One and a half weeks. That was a pain.

And from a customer from California:

> Say you are doing a refinance in today's market—your rate is one thing today but another thing tomorrow. If it takes very long to get approval, you could end up with a higher rate than you began with. Time is of the essence in a refinance.

This suggests that there exists a time dimension to responsiveness by the bank. Customers have some preconceived ideas about how long it should take a bank to answer their questions. Responsiveness means not only getting back to customers, but also doing so on their time schedule.

Responsiveness Means Solving Problems

Finally, responsiveness means solving problems for customers. For example, one customer from Illinois said:

> Bad service means not resolving problems. If you call on the telephone, for example, you'll end up talking to someone different each time you have a problem. And people often are uncaring and rude. People who don't like their jobs should not be in business.

And these two comments from customers in North Carolina and Colorado respectively:

> I am concerned about the lack of a "can do" attitude on the part of bankers. I only want to know how they can help me solve my problems, not what *their* problems are in solving mine.

> If I go into a bank and they can't solve my problem, I expect them to call someone else to help *right then!* As a customer, I do not want to have to come back later.

To these customers, the ability to solve problems efficiently and effectively determines service quality.

Summary—Responsiveness

The initial section of this chapter on the interpersonal relationship dimension of service quality has been concerned with defining, through customer insights, responsiveness. We have observed that, to the customers in our focus groups, responsiveness means such things as sensitivity, flexibility, going the extra mile, having a personal focus, following up with the customer, responding to needs in a timely fashion, and solving problems. It is obvious to us that responsiveness is multi-dimensional, with different meanings to different customers. The challenge for bankers is to determine what responsiveness means to their customers and design their banking organizations accordingly.

Courtesy

The second component of the interpersonal relationship dimension, following responsiveness, is courtesy. We found that courtesy comprises the subcomponents of friendliness, consideration, and respect for customers. To the extent that customers perceive a bank as possessing the traits of friendliness, consideration, and respect, that bank is considered to be courteous. To the extent these attributes are not perceived as being present, the bank is discourteous and therefore less likely to provide high-quality service.

Courtesy Means Friendliness

First, here are some comments from customers that lend definition to the idea of friendliness. A customer from New York commented:

> Years ago a bank in the Northeast had a saying, "You have a friend." A relative of mine was a corporate officer with a large company. It was raining outside. Her own bank was 10 blocks down the street, so she decided to go next door to this bank and cash a cashiers check. They would not cash it, and the woman behind the counter got a little abusive. My relative said, "I thought I had a friend here." The teller replied, "He died." My relative told a friend who had an account with this bank. The friend called the branch manager and cleared all the money out of her account.

This is an interesting situation because the bank, from the perspective of management, had decided that a competitive advantage was forthcoming from being friendly in its competitive environment. But apparently this was not communicated throughout the bank's hierarchy. One unfriendly transaction cost the bank a sizable account and untold future negative comments. Here the bank had, through advertising, created an expectation of friendliness in the customer's mind but did not follow through and make friendliness a reality.

A customer from Nebraska said:

> I do my commercial banking downtown on a daily basis, and I really look forward to coming down because the people are so friendly. It's just fantastic. I come in, and I really enjoy it. I now know everybody in the building. It's a friendly atmosphere whenever I walk in.

And another from Colorado said:

> I feel I get personal service when they take time to say things like "Have a Merry Christmas." I have never been at a bank more friendly than my bank. Even the ones who aren't waiting on you speak.

These customers look forward to making the trip to the bank because they know they will be greeted warmly and served by people who are friendly. This will not substitute for performing well on the other dimensions of service quality, such as accuracy. But it certainly can make instances of inaccuracy more palatable for customers and for the bank. One customer from California said:

> At my bank everybody from the president to the teller knows me by name. If I am putting big amounts or little amounts in, it is real nice to be known by name and asked, "How are you doing?"

This is interesting because we heard in North Carolina that calling a customer by name was not all that important. But, when investigating this further, it was found that *forced* name calling was viewed by customers as inappropriate. When the banker had to read the name from a check or other document, this was not viewed as being sincerely friendly. Apparently, it is easy for customers to spot insincerity.

But another customer from Mississippi does not object to her name being read from a check. She said:

> When I go into my branch, there are four or five people in there always just gushing to help me out. I think it is the friendliest place I have ever seen. It is important to be greeted and thanked. Nice to be called by name, even if they have to look at your check to know it.

And finally, a customer from Tennessee said:

> In all the different outlets that my bank has, I have never gone into one where they were grumpy. They always seemed happy.

Courtesy Means Being Considerate

The second component of courtesy is consideration. This concerns the degree to which the bank is willing to put itself in the position of customers and act accordingly. Consider this situation of a man from Louisiana:

> My husband and I decided we wanted to get a consolidation loan so that, rather than paying 14 to 15 small checks each month, we could just make one payment. Well, the bank officer had the gall to sit across the table from us and say, "I don't know how two young people like you could be so far into debt!" We were only talking about a $4,000 consolidation loan. We took our three accounts out of that bank and went somewhere else to do our business.

This banker, according to the customer, was not considerate of the customer's feelings and situation. The customer needed advice and help, not condescension.

Another lady, from California, gave this example of consideration:

> I called up and asked a question about my checking account because I couldn't get it to balance. The lady I talked to told me I needed to *hire* an accountant to get it straightened out! I didn't like that answer. Now, when I go in, she turns her head and ignores me. I don't like that at all.

What did the teller hope to gain by being inconsiderate of this customer's needs? Perhaps the teller just did not want to be bothered. We wonder if the teller even considered that the bank might have been in error, causing the balancing problem itself.

One man from North Carolina told the following story:

> My wife went to the drive-in window. She put her checks in the tray that comes out, and the teller left it open to turn around and talk to someone behind her. It was windy that day, and the checks blew out. The teller told my wife to go out and look for them. When she got the checks back, she went inside and closed the account.

It would not have taken much effort at least to help the customer recover the checks.

A customer from Illinois told this story:

> One bank I used to use did this: I went to get a large sum of money from my account. They wanted to know the reason I wanted to take the money out. I said, "That is none of your business. It is my money, and I want it." I had to come up with a reason, otherwise they said they wouldn't give me my money.

This customer viewed the request for a reason for a withdrawal to be inappropriate and inconsiderate. Customers tend to resent the prying some bankers insist upon when it comes to withdrawing funds. Most customers recognize the legitimate function of protecting their funds, but this practice must stop well short of intruding on their privacy.

Not all examples of consideration are negative. Listen to this woman from California:

> When I opened up my business account, I not only had a lot of money but also a lot of questions. The banker was so friendly with me. I had a little girl with me, and not only did she help keep the little girl occupied, but she also answered my questions and even offered to sell my product there at the branch. I was really pleased. That made me feel so good. It was really great. I went home to my husband and said, "You are not going to believe this."

Courtesy Means Respect for the Individual

The third and final subcomponent of courtesy is respect. By this, we mean respect for the customer as an individual and for the customer's business and personal financial needs no matter what they are.

Consider the following statement by a business customer from North Carolina:

> I used to be with one bank but left because they were not my kind of people. I don't know if you have ever been in this bank, but they greet you with a cup of coffee, sit you down in overstuffed chairs or on a couch, and give you a copy of *The Wall Street Journal* while you wait. There are no tellers. The guys that I hire are big, all jocks of one sort or another, and they don't take any grief from anybody. They would walk into the bank on a Friday afternoon in their paint-stained clothes. I was constantly getting phone calls asking, "Do you know this guy?" I would say yes, that I just gave him his paycheck. I was then told, "We do not want these kind of people in our lobby!" That was the end of my banking business. I explained to another bank what my people would look like on Friday afternoon and they still wanted my business.

This appears to demonstrate a lack of respect for the customer's business. It is the banker's job to get acquainted with the type of business the customer is in and to develop appropriate service outlets. It is not appropriate to question every check the customer writes to employees.

Another example of respect was offered by a customer from Mississippi:

> I do not think they realized what potential they had with me. Somewhere along the line, in a few years, I could have considerable money. I do not think they really know that or realize that people have potential. If you want "snoot," you go to a bank in London.

This demonstrates some lack of respect for the person or, in this case, the potential person that is in all of us.

And finally a positive story of respect from a woman from Nebraska:

> I was getting divorced and needed to open a checking account. I walked into a bank and said, "Can you tell me about your services?" The banker said, "Sure, come on in," and she had a lot of people there. She said, "Just a minute," and then took me in the back to a meeting room. I explained my situation and told her that I had a large amount of money to deposit with a bank. She explained ways to do it and called in another banker. They said if they could help me, just let them know. It was like a family attitude in there. When I went out the door, everybody was saying goodbye to me on a first-name basis.

Summary—Courtesy

As indicated by our customer focus group respondents, courtesy means different things to different people. We have observed that courtesy, in its principal components, means being friendly with the customer, being considerate, and respecting the customer as an individual. Again, your task is to determine what courtesy means to your customers and how to translate this meaning into habitual daily behavior by your employees.

Accessibility

The third component of the interpersonal relationship dimension is what we identify as accessibility. Again, this means different things to different people. But, generally, our research suggests that accessibility means two things to most bank customers. First, accessibility means being approachable. Is the bank structured for ease of approach by customers? Are personnel easily approached, and does that approach yield a pleasant experience for customers? Second, accessibility means availability. Are the services of the bank and the banker available at times of the customers' needs? This means having a network of service outlets available for customers to use when they want to use them.

Accessible Means Being Approachable

To begin, let us consider the expectation of a customer from California. This statement is not inconsistent with the tone of comments we heard around the country:

> My banker should be *completely* accessible. This means all the time when I need the banker through whatever means necessary.

As an example of approachable, consider the following comment from a customer from Idaho:

> My bank is a success because it strives for personal service. The ability to get in to see a key officer who would eventually make a decision is made easier. It is extremely accessible. I certainly appreciate this. If you put a request in for something, you get action on it in a relatively short period of time.

The bank had designed a system whereby the customer was comfortable in approaching a key officer and having a transaction completed.

A customer from California said this:

> My bank is definitely service-oriented and will do just about anything for you. This has to do with the direction established by the president right on down the line. If there is a line, someone who is not a teller will get up from their chair and see if they can help. And even after hours, if I knock on the door somebody will come and see if they can help me.

This indicates that approachable begins at the top of the hierarchy. If the CEO/President communicates approachability, the employees are likely to do so too.

Another customer, from Colorado, told of the importance of a personal relationship when defining accessibility:

> If my bank changes managers, the new manager ought to at least come see me and introduce himself. I must be able to access someone when I need them. I like dealing with a small bank where I can get a one-on-one relationship with a banker knowing my needs and do not always have to go through a committee.

How important it is to allow customers the comfort to approach someone who will help with their financial needs! The bank creates this atmosphere but can also easily destroy it.

A customer formerly from Texas relates how the structure of the banking system can harm approachability:

> I don't like branch banking. I guess that's because I am from Texas. It is pretty hard to get to know anyone in the branch banking systems. I go to a loan officer and really do not think he is capable of lending me money. He has to go to a committee for a decision. In Texas I could go directly to a loan officer and get a loan—no committee.

This does not necessarily mean that ease of approach cannot be designed into branch banking systems, but it may be more difficult to do so. Management, therefore, must expend greater effort to see that ease of approach happens in a branch banking environment.

Again, an example of the personal relationship in determining ease of approach was described by a customer in North Carolina:

> I will not make a deposit unless I can walk in and hand it to a teller. I enjoy going into the hank and saying hello.

And, as a message to larger banks, one customer from California said:

> The larger the organization, the more layers of personnel you have to go through to get an answer.

But does this have to be? Why can't a large organization be designed to allow for ease of approach by customers? We think so—if the necessary effort is spent on organizational design, structure, and processes.

And finally, perhaps the ultimate personal response to ease of approach comes from a customer in Mississippi:

> My banker prints his home phone number on his business cards. Now that is real accessibility.

If you want to send a direct and strong message to your customers about being approachable and accessible, try that.

Accessibility Means Being Available

The second component of accessibility that we identified was availability. Being available means having branches, ATMs, and points of inquiry designed into a banking system to make the services easily available to customers. It also means having people available for assistance, according to one customer from Nebraska:

> My bank has a 1-800 assistance number, and it is located out of state. It is just answering *off* a computer, and it couldn't care less. When I was able to deal with people locally, I liked it much better.

This was viewed as an impersonal and inadequate substitute for local, personal assistance.

Another example, from a Florida customer, shows that merely having the service available is not enough. It must then be delivered:

> Bad service, to me, means inconvenience. Waiting and waiting to make a transaction. Sometimes teller lines are 30 deep. That is just mismanagement.

And another added:

> I know a situation that is very bad. There are about 20 teller windows and only four are open. I really get upset over this. Talk about service—that is the worst way to operate a bank.

And a customer from Mississippi tells how selling sometimes gets in the way of the availability of service:

> Some banks give quotas to their tellers to sell so much. I feel that sometimes they are compromising service because they are trying to sell a CD, etcetera. Those who only want to get their daily banking done have to wait. I believe in selling products, but I believe the actual service is compromised.

Having service available means not letting the customer know that the computers are down, according to this California customer:

> It seems like, whenever the computers go down, there should be some backup. I was out at night going to catch a plane and was going to stop at the ATM. I drove to four different machines before I found one that was working.

To a customer in Nebraska, being available means having necessary information when and where the customer needs it.

> Accessibility means availability of information: being able to call one number and get information without being transferred five times. I do not have time to go to the bank, so I will call to find out something.

Another aspect of availability is having the type of delivery wanted by the customer, as evidenced by one customer in Illinois:

> I look for convenience and low cost or no cost. I try to stay out of the bank. I make my deposits by mail or electronically, and I have very minimal need to go to a bank. I mean *convenient* not in terms of location, but in terms of, say, ATMs. I do not really care where the bank is located as long as I can get my money when I need it.

Summary—Accessibility

As with the other dimensions of quality of service from the customer's perspective, accessibility is rather complex, consisting of several parts. For example, accessibility may mean any one or a combination of a location close to home or office, the availability of an ATM, availability of mail-in banking services, hours open, ease of contact by phone, lack of phone transfers to have a question answered or a problem dealt with, and home phone numbers of personal bankers. All of these components of accessibility, and there may be others, must work together to yield ease of access to banking services for each consumer.

Summary

This chapter has considered the interpersonal relationship dimension of service quality. Our work found that establishing good relationships means being responsive, courteous, and accessible to customers. This is the dimension where the bank makes the commitment to respond to individual customer needs within a framework of courteous and friendly relationships. Bankers, according to our findings, need to be accessible on the customers' terms, not necessarily on terms established by the bankers.

Chapter

The Dimension of Knowing Customers

Our work has indicated that banks which concentrate on ensuring that every organizational element contributing to customer satisfaction—e.g., product development, distribution, sales messages, employee attitudes, after-sales follow-up, grievance resolution, incentives, and tangible symbols of service—are unswervingly focused on the same goal of superior customer satisfaction at a profit. We believe that customer satisfaction is the result of the relationship between bank performance and customer expectations, with customer expectations being the primary factor in the relationship. The extent to which the bank is interested in knowing its customers determines how well it knows their expectations. The dimension of knowing customers can be divided into two subcomponents: understanding the customers and communicating with them.

Understanding

In determining service quality, the bank must seek to meld its organizational mind with the customer mind to become one in service. The melding of minds comes down to understanding the customer, but what exactly does this mean?

Understanding Means Learning the Individual's Needs

Understanding customers means making the effort to deal with them as individuals, even if the customers are businesses, in determining what they want and need. Oftentimes, customers do not fully understand their own needs or which bank services may satisfy those needs. So, the bank must know and understand its customers well enough to direct them in the proper way. A comment from a customer in Nebraska is illustrative:

> I'm all for the friendly, courteous service. In that business you have to be a "people person," (or at least) you should be a people person. You are there to serve your customers and their needs to the best of your ability. I think that is really important because so many people end up with accounts they don't need or the wrong kind of accounts. You need to get to know your customers. You need best to suit an individual need.

This is indicative of what we heard across the United States. Customers expect their financial institutions to know them and best to suit their individual needs.

Another customer, from North Carolina, told this story:

> If it has a good customer, the bank should know who he is. I bounced two checks because of a mistake. My statement got charged $18.00. I was notified by mail. Why didn't they call me and let me know of a problem? That irritates me. They didn't tell me for two days that there was a mistake or problem. I bounced a check with one of my vendors. The vendor may not do business with me again, all because that bank didn't understand what the consequences would be for me. If they had known me, a good customer, they could have helped me avoid

this problem. But they probably thought "We'll get him now for making a mistake."

It is true that the previous example contains elements of communicating with customers, which we will consider in the next section. But the customer himself described the situation as one of not understanding him and his business enough to react with sensitivity to his problem. He viewed the bank as just trying to get two checks out of the processing system as quickly as possible rather than taking the time to understand the consequences of bouncing the checks of an historically good customer. Good customers should be valued and dealt with accordingly because they are the franchise.

Another customer from North Carolina said:

> The branch manager at the bank where I have my business account came to my business to see if everything was all right. I was very impressed that he came to my store. Now, unless the bank really messes up, I'm a customer for life. He talks to his customers. He showed me that he wants my business. He is willing to take his time to develop an understanding of me and my business. I feel appreciated by his walking in that door. This is my most positive experience with a bank.

This brings up an interesting point. First, the time devoted to getting to know and understand customers is well spent. However, it is not entirely sufficient in providing service quality. The customer noted that the bank must still perform if he is to remain a customer. That is, performance must take place within the framework of knowing customers for high-quality service to be forthcoming.

Understanding Means Personal Attention and Involvement

The customers we talked to also seek a bank that will give them personal attention, expending the bank's time and effort. They also expect active involvement by the bank in getting to understand their situation and needs. This means being proactive in initiating service encounters rather than waiting for the customer to do so. Regarding this, a customer from California had this comment:

> I'm a furrier, and I buy things I've been told not to buy. I bought on feel, while they would buy on expertise; and in many cases I was buying as a customer, not as a furrier.
>
> Whether you are a furrier, a banker, or whatever, if you get to the point where you are working with numbers only, you will lose perspective. We deal with customers. I think so often banks have forgotten that they are dealing with the people and not just numbers.

Customers are not transactions. Customers have transactions; but they are individuals with different needs, wants, and time horizons that must be understood to be served effectively.

A customer from Colorado said:

> I consider a large bank an "institution." They don't know me and they are faceless to me, too. But the bank where I do all my loan business, they know me. That bank I don't call an institution. So I think the main difference is how well they *want* to get to know me and my needs. I think the larger the less personal.

We wonder why we heard this theme across the country. We can think of no compelling reason why bigness *must* mean less personal. Apparently, bigness implies less personal in the perceptual world of customers. Our analysis, however, questions the inevitability of this. A large bank can organize to be personal, even if it is harder to do than in a small bank. We reject the notion that large must mean impersonal. But it does take effort not to be impersonal, regardless of the size of the bank.

Another customer, from Nebraska, told of this situation:

> When my father was 89 (he is now 94) he lived in a senior high rise. He loved to do things for other people. He could walk the six blocks down the street to do his banking. He found that one of his lady friends had a bad leg and couldn't walk that far.

He offered to deposit her check for her when he did his banking. The bank was nice enough to accept the fact that he was being nice to someone else, and they were flexible enough to let him do her banking. He did this regularly tor her. It was a convenience for her, and it pleased him that the bank trusted him.

Maybe this was not good, traditional banking practice in terms of security. But that bank afforded sensitivity and personal attention to two customers. It was meaningful to the customer's father and to one of his friends that the bank would focus personally on their special banking requirements.

And from a Mississippi customer:

When I go in a bank, I feel I want the people I deal with to have an interest in what I'm talking about and help *me,* actually, with *my* problem.

The operative records to that customer are *me and my*. Deal with me personally, with your time and effort, was the message.

And finally, to gain perspective in dealing with the public, listen to a customer from New York:

Whenever you're dealing with the public, you have to look at the customer and think, "How would I respond if I were that person." Banks don't do this very well.

Many customers believe that banks typically respond from their own perspective rather than from the customers. We, too, find this in many situations. We held a seminar on service quality recently where we focused on what customers expected from banks. We found many banks wanting to argue about why they could not respond to customer wishes in many situations. Many such arguments involved limitations created by current systems. Our answer was that systems must be designed to respond to customer needs, not banks' convenience.

Understanding Means
Recognizing the Regular Customer

Perhaps one of the most important needs in the lives of most people is the need to be recognized and accepted by others. We believe this is true and significant for bank customers. Furthermore, it is important for the bank to create the setting in which customers are recognized and accepted as individuals. This is communicated by a customer from North Carolina who said:

> I can go into my branch bank. My daughter left to go to New York four months ago, and the manager and another employee remember her. She only banked there for six months. Now they'll ask, "How is your daughter doing?" It's nice. They remember people.

This customer was convinced that his bank was special because it remembered his daughter after only a short exposure to her.

And a customer from California said:

> It's very important to me that they know who I am when I call. I also look for flexibility.

It is even important to customers that they be recognized when they call, not just when they walk into the bank. This is evidenced by another customer in California, who said:

> It is calling up and saying, "I am your customer, and can you give me my balance in my account?" And I do not have to give them my great grandmother's blood type, because they know who I am. At my bank I do not have to give an account number. They know me.

And finally, a customer from North Carolina told this story:

> I used to bank with another bank. When I first went with them, they were small. Everybody knew you. You would walk in and have your name called. Then they kept getting bigger and bigger, and then somebody bought them out. You know the story. So I moved my accounts.

Many times customers feel lost in the bank merger activity that has occurred over the past few years and is still occurring. They told us that they felt bank management was more driven by corporate ownership concern than by customer satisfaction concerns. This is unfortunate from a consumer perspective. Even in merger situations, consumers expect to be recognized as good customers, no matter who has current ownership.

Summary—Understanding

In summary, we believe the first subcomponent of knowing customers—understanding—means learning the individual's specific needs, giving personal attention and involvement, and recognizing the regular customer. The bank that performs these well will have made a good beginning toward understanding the customer.

Communicating

The second aspect of knowing the customer is communicating. As with understanding, communicating comprises several subcomponents.

Communicating Means Keeping Customers Informed

Many customers indicated to us that they needed to be kept better informed about issues that affected their financial status. They should be kept informed not only about the activities of their bank, but also about the general movement of financial concerns when they could potentially benefit from knowing. In the following statement, a customer from North Carolina equates bad service specifically with lack of information. He said:

> Bad quality is lack of information and not being able to get to what I need or want. I had a situation not long ago where I had two bank accounts that I was trying to consolidate into one. The bank, without my knowledge, took a line of credit off one account and added it to the other account. I received no

information about this at all. When I went to the bank to find out about it, I was told, "I do not know. I can't find out, but here is a number for you to call." I got an answer when I called, but I wanted to talk to someone face to face—that is why I *went* to the bank to get an answer. I felt like they really were not interested in talking with me.

The bank, the customer felt, had made a unilateral decision involving him but did not bother to communicate it. The customer was not upset with the bank for dealing with the line of credit. But he was upset with not being told that this was happening. Is this an isolated event? Apparently not, considering the number of similar comments that ensued.

One customer from New York told the following story about lack of communicating:

I was irritated at first by not getting my checks back in my checking statement; but, on reflection, I suppose it really doesn't matter that much as long as my checks are accessible. But it irritated me, because I wasn't told this change had been made. I just got my statement and no checks. The big difference was they didn't tell me ahead of time.

Again, that customer was entirely willing to accept no return of canceled checks as long as his checks were accessible. However, the bank chose not to inform the customer of the change but simply imposed the change. This was a source of irritation. An irritated customer will not easily be convinced of good service quality. A customer from Mississippi gave the following example:

Recently I sent a sizable check to my broker. It represented the rollover from a bank IRA certificate that was maturing in a week. My broker had instructions to hold the check until a certain date and then, after I deposited the maturing CD into my checking account, he would deposit my check into his account. Well, you guessed it. The broker did not tell his staff, and the check was immediately deposited. The first I learned of it was by mail when I received an overdraft notice that my account was $20,000 overdrawn. I'm a good customer of the bank, and they paid this check rather than returning it to the broker. Now, I appreciated the fact that the bank paid the check. But this transaction was so out of the ordinary relative to my checking account that I would view personal service as calling me on the phone and asking me about the check. In this particular case, I would have instructed the bank to return the check to the broker. It would have saved me $200 in overdraft charges. All they had to do was communicate with me and let me make the decision, not make it for me.

This is an interesting issue because the bank, in trying to provide very good service, actually provided poor service relative to communicating with the customer. This could have been prevented with a single phone call.

Another information issue was raised by a Nebraska customer:

I didn't know my bank had merged with a larger one until I looked across the street and saw the sign. This merger was real cheap so far as informing customers.

We realize that merger negotiations are very sensitive and must be kept confidential. But we also realize the need of customers to know what is happening to the institution to which they have entrusted a portion of their future. Perhaps an immediate letter to existing customers would be in order. It certainly would be preferable to having them find out they are doing business with a different bank by seeing a new sign being raised.

Another customer, from Texas, thinks that banks should address good and bad in communicating with customers:

You always learn good news through advertising, but the bad news with reducing interest on savings isn't publicized like good news. You almost have to discover it on your own. It seems you don't hear the bad news as clearly as the good news that they want you to hear.

We do not think it is in the long-term best interest of banks to reduce customer exposure to bad news. But explain the news in terms the customer can understand. If you reduce rates on CDs, customers want to know up front so they can exercise control over their financial activities. And if keeping customers informed provides bad results for the bank, maybe the bank should consider lowering its rates.

One customer from California was furious with something that is fairly routine. He said:

> Recently my bank pulled something on me that I did not appreciate. They sold my mortgage to another financial institution that I never heard of. I think they should have notified me before they did that. I got a letter from the mortgage company telling me they had my mortgage. My bank never notified me at all. They should have as far as I am concerned.

Not all customers know that mortgages can be sold. They do not necessarily object to this practice, but they object strenuously to not being told by the bank.

Communicating Means Using Customer Language

Customers are not familiar with financial terminology. Oftentimes bankers use "in-group" language, just as if everyone were as informed as they are about financial products. In the following statement, a customer from Mississippi states the need to use customer language:

> Sometimes it seems I have to read so many different columns on my statement to see what's what. I would like to see it very easy. I know what checks I have deposited. I know how much money I had there. I know what was deducted. I know what the balance is—just real easy. Not having to search through how the figures did this and that. I don't care if a check got there in sequence or not. It either got there or didn't get there. I just want to know what my balance is. To me they make them as complicated as they can, trying to tell me everything. I really don't care. Good quality of service is communicating with me so I can understand it.

Everything that is used to communicate with customers in your bank, from phone communication to billboards, should be designed and stated in terms that customers can readily understand without a financial interpreter. Another example of communicating with the customer comes from North Carolina:

> If a bank tells me something that I think is absolutely stupid, they should explain it to me. Here is an example. I took a check to the bank that was made out to my mortgage company. I am the sole owner of the company. I thought, "Oh, here is a little pocket money." I asked the teller to cash it. I said, "I am the company, you know that. "Well, let me explain," she answered. "We know you're the company, but we do not know whether maybe you have a silent partner who is entitled to 50 percent of this check. Now, we can cash it. But if that partner ever got wind of it, he could come in and we would be in a heap of trouble." I said, "Say no more." She explained it and I understood.

This indicates the need to explain bank policy to customers so they understand fully the rationale behind the policy. Most people accept the explanations if they are presented in terms they can understand.

Communicating Means Initiating Contact

Many customers expressed concern that they always seemed to initiate the contact with the bank. Perhaps this is the established way of doing business. But many customers wished to have the bank initiate the contact when it was in the best interest of the customer for the bank to do so. For example, a customer from California said:

> My bank calls me to see how I am doing and how they are doing things for me. Of course they would call if I was upset about something, but they will call just to be sure I am happy.

This demonstrates active interest by initiating a point of contact with the customer. It gives the banker the opportunity to express herself to the customer, and it gives the customer an opportunity for expression to the bank that is not clouded by a transaction.

One customer from Colorado said:

> My bank had a change in its minimum balance requirement, but this was hidden down in a page of typing. This is a very poor way to advise customers of a change in their checking accounts.

The implication from that customer was that the bank could change the minimum balance requirement if it wanted, but "Tell me first and do not hide it in a page of print. Tell me up front."

And a customer from North Carolina indicated a relationship between being kept informed and initiating contact:

> Until my bank was sold, I would have said friendliness meant quality. But now it would be *being kept informed.* When there are changes in the way things are being done, I would like to know about them—they have my money. My money is very important to me and I don't know what is happening to it. So being kept informed is good-quality service. I got a phone call from one of my bankers who had picked up a deposit I made last night in the night depository. He said he was just calling to let me know I had shorted myself by $10, and he made the adjustment for me. That is the first phone call I ever had from someone at the bank. I appreciated it.

Customers appreciate calls from their banks if they are calls that indicate service. They are not especially appreciative of "sales" calls unless such calls are made to communicate a personalized service the customer can use or may need.

The following two examples indicate the need to initiate contact with customers before designing statements and other forms of formal items by which the bank communicates. First from a Colorado customer:

> I have accounts with a bank, and I get one sheet of paper each month. On this is listed everything I do at the bank: savings, checking, IRA, CDs. Everything is listed there telling me what I have. It tells me everything I want to know, what I am doing at that bank monthly.

And from a North Carolina customer:

> I have a savings account and an IRA at my bank. I like to get monthly statements showing deposits, interest, and maturity dates. But now I only get this once a year, and I do not like it.

Summary—Communicating

These examples indicate the importance of formal communications to customers and how each type can be indicative of service quality. The bank must find the most appropriate way to communicate with customers and respond accordingly.

Communicating with customers means letting them know about issues of importance to them and their banking relationship. It means doing so in language the customers readily understand. An important component of communication, we believe, is initiating contact with customers. Banks should become more proactive and actually seek out opportunities to communicate with their customers, rather than wait for customers to make the first contact.

Summary

This chapter has discussed the quality of service dimension of knowing customers. While nearly every bank with which we made contact expressed knowledge of its customers, most customers expressed the desire for their bankers to know them better. When a banker knew an individual, whether through a personal or business relationship, the banker was better equipped to meet the unique expectations of that individual. This knowledge is also translated into actionable quality when good communication channels are open and readily accessible by both parties—bank and customer. Knowing your customer thoroughly is an absolute requirement for establishing a high-quality service relationship.

What follows are four in-depth examples of banks that made the customer the driving force in the way they do business. We have selected these four banks not only because of the outstanding customer service that they offer, but because they use a customer service strategy to accomplish different goals. The first bank you will read about is the Bank of Yazoo City, a small community bank that has given new meaning to the idea of customer service. Concord Commercial Bank is an outstanding service deliverer providing top-notch service to businesses in the San Francisco area. Seafirst Bank uses customer service as a full distribution strategy in their Northwest markets, while Northern Trust leverages their expertise in customer service to reach the upscale markets. While each bank has a different strategic thrust, they are all exceptional examples of how banks can compete using a customer service approach.

Chapter

6

Customer Service the Yazoo City Way

The Bank of Yazoo City, founded in the city for which it was named, is located in the Mississippi Delta, a place famed for antebellum mansions, Southern hospitality, beautiful women, cotton, and exceptionally hot and humid summers. In 1876, a group of cotton merchants started the bank as a source of funds for their planting. Since that time, the Bank of Yazoo City, BYC, has survived a major depression and continually tough economic times, closing only for the bank holiday, and has ultimately become an $84 million bank.

Yazoo City, Mississippi (population 12,500) is located in Yazoo County (population 27,000). This part of Mississippi is heavily dependent upon agriculture and transfer payments. The local market is dominated by one relatively large company, Mississippi Chemical, which employs about 600 people. The customer base for banks operating in this market is heavily polarized with a significant wealthy segment and an equally significant "less affluent" population. Because of continually tough economic times, the middle income market has diminished considerably. Most descriptions of the area would include the word "poor." Bank management had looked at alternative geographic markets, but demographics in contiguous Delta counties are not conducive for expansion. To the South of Yazoo County, is Jackson, Mississippi, the capital of the state and the site of perhaps the most intensive banking competition in the state. As a result, Griffin Norquist, President of BYC, adopted his single market strategy, somewhat reminiscent of the Gerber baby food strategy—"Yazoo County is our business, our only business."

Three banks compete for the static, if not actually declining market that comprises Yazoo City. One bank is a branch of a $3 billion bank, the state's largest, while the other is a community bank with a branch in the local market. The Bank of Yazoo City controls in excess of 40% of their market, occupying a major position in the upscale market.

Rethinking BYC's Strategy

The BYC has enjoyed solid profitability in recent years in large part by focusing on the carriage trade and serving the local market as a home town bank. A conservative lending image and a reputation for serving only wealthy customers have been both a blessing and a problem for current bank management. Van Ray, Senior Vice President of BYC, acknowledges this image and admits that for years, "the bank had turned away the low-end checking account. We had a $1500 rule and no checking meant no loans."

However, this policy has put the BYC at some risk creating an overreliance on one market segment that has an average age of 56, an undiversified loan portfolio, and a relatively high cost of funds. Ray characterized the bank as follows:

> BYC is basically a commercial bank that needs to move more
> to the retail side of the business. Everything around here is

agriculture or involves businesses that are ag-related. We were heavily invested into agricultural lending. In 1984, out of a $30 million loan portfolio, only $2 million was in the consumer market. We needed to increase our consumer loan business. It is more stable and is proving to be a very profitable business. Now our consumer loans comprise about 27% of our loan portfolio, up from the 7% figure in 1984.

This strategic shift is somewhat impeded by BYC's image and the presence of a powerful competitor for the retail customer across the street. The scale of operations of the major competitor combined with the quality of its management make it an imposing obstacle to market diversification. Impelling the management of BYC, however, is a realization that they can not compete against the product development and product delivery capabilities of this larger bank. Again, Ray articulated this competitive reality when he said the following:

> We know we can't compete with them product-by-product. They have a large marketing staff and a huge budget. They can come up with all the innovation they want to and we can not compete with them. We will always be in a follower position. A while back we tried to market a home equity loan product in response to their product. We spent $5,000 developing the product only to find out that there was no real market for it. We had to find some other approach to the market that was available to us.

The Strategic Shift

BYC's strategic shift started in 1987 when an efficiency expert was brought in to streamline the bank. The thrust of this effort was cost containment. The results of this program were mixed. On the one hand, BYC was able to lower their costs of doing business but only at the expense of employee morale. Over 300 changes were made in the bank. Everyone was moved physically. The changes were effected in such a way that employees were afraid for their jobs and, what was characterized by several of the tellers as a "bad internal situation" developed. In 1988 Griffin Norquist took over as President of BYC having inherited a questionable strategic outlook and a less than favorable employee situation.

After a period of stabilization, Norquist began a strong move to become more of a retail bank. At the heart of this move was the objective of not just good customer service but providing the best service that could be found in the market area! Behind this decision is what Norquist articulated as his "Wal-Mart theory of banking." Norquist explained that the situation facing local small town merchants who are confronted with the opening of a Wal-Mart in their local market is very similar to that of a smaller, local, independent bank who has to compete against the branch of a large statewide system. However, Norquist believes that there is a certain strength in being a local independent bank. He explained:

> In small Southern towns, this may be true elsewhere, when a Wal-Mart comes it destroys downtown business. I knew there had to be some way for small businesses to compete with Wal-Mart. The exact same thing is true in banking where you are an independent bank. In the South, and again, perhaps elsewhere, there is some loyalty to the independent local bank. But I also knew that this would not bring us through the times profitably and continue to make us profitable. How would I approach the Wal-Marts of banking? Our Wal-Mart is right across the street from us. Our major competitor is a $3 billion bank whose headquarters are less than 40 miles away. *I could either approach it like many small town businesses approach Wal-Mart—'We'll just do the best we can and try to hang in there' or we could become very aggressive on quality.* There is no way we can compete with them on price or product. We have an advantage even if our mega competitor moves to a quality strategy. Our advantage lies in a senior management that is in the bank trying to find out if the customer is being treated the way he or she should be treated. That is key. The quality of our service is further enhanced when senior management is out of our offices and out in the lobby!

Survey Results Showed
BYC to Be Well Positioned

The BYC had always enjoyed a good reputation for service so Norquist knew that he was not starting from ground zero. A study of customer perceptions from BYC and their competitors was conducted. Four hundred residents of Yazoo County, the BYC market area, were surveyed over the phone concerning their perceptions of banking and the quality of service that they were receiving from their primary financial institution. Figure 6-1 is a sample of the survey used.

Figure 6-1
Customer Service Survey

Hello, my name is _____. I'm calling for Telemarketing, Inc. We are conducting a survey on banks. May I please speak to the person who handles banking for your family? Thank you. Do you or anyone in your family work for a bank? (If yes, thank them and discontinue the survey. If no, continue.) Do you do any banking in Yazoo City? (If no, thank them and discontinue the survey. If yes, continue.)

1. What is your primary bank in Yazoo City?
   _____ Bank of Yazoo City
   _____
   _____
   _____
   _____ other _____

2. How satisfied are you with the quality of service you get from your bank?
   _____ very satisfied
   _____ satisfied
   _____ neither satisfied nor dissatisfied
   _____ dissatisfied
   _____ very dissatisfied
   _____ don't know/no opinion

3. Would you say that your bank gives you good service:
   _____ always
   _____ sometimes
   _____ seldom
   _____ never
   _____ don't know/no opinion

Figure 6-1
Customer Service Survey *continued*

4. Would you say that your bank is too big, the right size, or too
    small to give you the kind of service you need?
    _____ too big
    _____ the right size
    _____ too small
    _____ don't know/no opinion

Now I'm going to read some statements that may describe your bank.
Please tell me if you agree or disagree. (If the respondent agrees, ask
if they strongly agree or just agree. SA means strongly agree, A
means agree, N means neutral, D means disagree, SD means strongly
disagree, DK means don't know. Please circle the answer.)

5. My bank consistently
    gives me good service.   SA A N D SD DK
6. My bank is responsive
    to my needs as a customer.   SA A N D SD DK
7. My bank cares about me
    as a customer.   SA A N D SD DK
8. The services at my bank
    cost less than the services
    of other banks in town.   SA A N D SD DK
9. My bank offers the
    services I need.   SA A N D SD DK
10. I enjoy going to my bank.   SA A N D SD DK
11. The tellers at my bank are
    friendly.   SA A N D SD DK
12. I would recommend my
    bank to family members
    and friends.   SA A N D SD DK
13. It is convenient for me to
    do business with my bank.   SA A N D SD DK
14. My bank does what it says
    it will do in its advertising. SA A N D SD DK
15. My bank treats me like an
    important customer.   SA A N D SD DK
16. My bank understands my
    banking needs.   SA A N D SD DK
17. My bank does not make
    mistakes in handling my
    business.   SA A N D SD DK

Figure 6-1
Customer Service Survey *continued*

18. I feel secure doing
    business with my bank.   SA A N D SD DK
19. My bank makes it easy
    for me to do my banking
    business there.   SA A N D SD DK
20. I would switch banks if I
    could get better service at
    another bank in town.   SA A N D SD DK

So far we have been talking about _____, which you said is
your primary bank in Yazoo City. Now I'd like to get your opinion
about another bank.

21. If you were to bank somewhere else in Yazoo City, which
    bank would you choose?
    _____ Bank of Yazoo City
    _____ Bank 1
    _____ Bank 2
    _____ Bank 3
    _____ other (name)_____
    _____ don't know/no opinion
22. How would you rate the quality of service _____
    gives its customers? (Use name of bank given in question 21.)
    _____ very good
    _____ good
    _____ average
    _____ bad
    _____ very bad
    _____ don't know/no opinion
23. Would you describe the customers who bank there as:
    _____ upper income
    _____ middle income
    _____ lower income
    _____ upper and middle income
    _____ middle and lower income
    _____ all three
    _____ don't know/no opinion

Figure 6-1
Customer Service Survey *continued*

Please tell me if you agree or disagree with the following
statements about _____. (Use the name of the bank given in
question 21.)

24. _____ provides the ser–
    vices I would need and
    use if I were a customer.   SA   A   N   D   SD   DK
25. If I banked at _____, it
    would be convenient for
    me.   SA   A   N   D   SD   DK
26. _____ charges more for
    its services than other
    banks in town.   SA   A   N   D   SD   DK
27. Of all the banks in Yazoo City, which bank is easiest to deal
    with when you need to borrow money?
    _____ Bank of Yazoo City
    _____ Bank 1
    _____ Bank 2
    _____ Bank 3
    _____ other _____
    _____ don't know/no opinion
28. Of all the banks in Yazoo City, which bank is most difficult
    to deal with when you need to borrow money?
    _____ Bank of Yazoo City
    _____ Bank 1
    _____ Bank 2
    _____ Bank 3
    _____ other _____
    _____ don't know/no opinion
29. If you needed to borrow money, is there a bank in Yazoo City
    that you would not go to?
    _____ Bank of Yazoo City
    _____ Bank 1
    _____ Bank 2
    _____ Bank 3
    _____ other _____
    _____ don't know/no opinion

Figure 6-1
Customer Service Survey *continued*

Now we are almost finished. These last few questions are for
classification purposes only.

30. gender:

    _____ male
    _____ female

31. race:

    _____ white
    _____ black
    _____ no response

32. age group

    _____ under 21
    _____ 21 to 29
    _____ 30 to 39
    _____ 40 to 49
    _____ 50 to 59
    _____ 60 and older
    _____ no response

33. income group

    _____ under $10,000
    _____ 10,000 to 19,999
    _____ 20,000 to 29,999
    _____ 30,000 to 39,999
    _____ 40,000 to 49,999
    _____ 50,000 and over
    _____ no response

This concludes our survey. Thank you for your cooperation.

The results of this survey provided some valuable insight into
how BYC management might move toward their objective of
greater penetration of the retail market as the premier customer
service bank. The key results of the survey indicated:

1. Among all customers, the BYC enjoyed a very good reputation for customer service. On most of the perceptions
   measured, BYC customers rated their bank higher than did
   the customers of competing institutions.

2. As a second choice bank, the BYC was rated higher than its
   competition. When customers were asked which bank they

would choose if they were to switch banks, the BYC was the top bank.

3. The BYC had a strong image as the most expensive bank and for serving the more wealthy segment. This finding substantiated the beliefs of senior management, a legacy of their past strategy.

4. An analysis of those customers who said that they would be willing to switch banks if they could get better service from another bank provided some of the most important information. First, potential switchers rated their bank's quality of service significantly lower than did other customers. Second, a demographic profile of the potential switchers revealed that they were skewed toward the lower end of the economic spectrum with a median income of between $20,000 and $30,000. These were prime candidates for the BYC. Third, "potential switchers" tended to be younger and fell into the profile of borrowers. Finally, the majority of the potential switchers were customers of the large bank, the branch of the statewide system—Norquist's Wal-Mart!

5. The survey indicated that a demonstrable sense of caring about customers was the most important factor determining an individual's willingness to recommend the bank to another. Of secondary importance was having available the necessary services, followed by a sense of responsiveness on the part of the bank, the friendliness of tellers, and a sense of security. This was an important finding in the survey since the BYC had a relatively small marketing budget compared to its major competitor. In addition, the availability of ad vehicles in the Yazoo County area is limited. Thus, information regarding those service factors that impacted positive word of mouth communications became even more important. Moreover, Norquist felt that the key to promoting the customer service strategy was "customers selling customers."

6. A similar analysis was performed on the customer's perception of the satisfaction with the quality of service received from his or her bank. Most important in influencing

this reaction was the idea of consistency of service. Friendliness of tellers, a sense of caring, having the necessary services, and minimizing mistakes all followed in importance.

Based on this information, the management of BYC developed a customer service strategy that could be communicated in a single statement.

**At Bank of Yazoo City, we're committed
to quality, value, and customer service.**

A single strategy statement was chosen for several reasons. First it was easy to communicate to bank staff. The strategy statement is printed on signs, appears at teller positions, is displayed on the desks of officers, and is apparent on all promotional materials. It is simple, easy to remember, and constantly visible throughout the bank. It is also a simple statement that customers can understand and contains three basic values: quality, value, and customer service. Finally, it represents a kind of standard that bank employees can gauge their own behavior against. Are they delivering quality? Are they delivering value? Are they delivering customer service?

One way of discounting the higher priced bank image was to add value to the basic banking products. Greater value, if perceived on the part of customers, conceptually reduced the price paid for the product or service. In this case, BYC was beefing up the value of the basic banking product with a heavy dose of high quality customer service.

Based on the research, management felt that they were ready to develop a plan to implement their customer service strategy. *Their objective was to increase their retail base through a top notch customer service delivery system.* Their target was the "working man" segment, specifically the individual who was willing to switch banks for better customer service. Realistically, BYC management understood that they would not be experiencing a flood of new customers simply because they advertised superior customer service. Rather, the implementation of the strategy involved demonstrating the high quality of customer service available at the bank, and becoming the alternative bank when a customer was ready to switch. Their current rank as the number one alternative gave them a solid base on which to build the "preferred alternative" bank. Management was committed to taking a slow, conservative approach to growth.

Putting Quality, Value, and Customer Service into Practice

A critical factor in the successful implementation of the BYC customer service strategy was the idea of empowering the employees to provide the service levels necessary to make the strategy work. Two objectives were identified for the training sessions. The first objective was to increase the customer interaction skills of the bank employees and management. In order to back their claim of not just good customer service but outstanding customer service, senior management focused on empowering the employees with the ability to deliver the best customer service possible.

The second objective addressed the relationship between how employees treated each other and how they treated customers. The basic premise behind this training impetus was the idea that high levels of customer service could only be delivered by people who respected each other, were committed to their jobs, and wanted to put the quality and value into the customer relationship. The earlier changes in the bank had left a legacy of mistrust and poor communication among the employees. There was little sense of teamwork and cooperation.

Supervisors were exposed to 36 hours of training, while employees received 24 hours. As part of the training, the idea of quality circles was introduced to the bank. Bank employees were exposed to how their ideas on how to serve the customer could be used to improve the overall customer service delivery system of the bank. By integrating quality circles within the training portion of the process, employees could gain experience on how to interact with each other and how to go about problem solving.

The following is a program description taken from BYC's customer service training. Figure 6-2 is an actual training program outline.

Program Description—Customer Service Training

The habitual delivery of excellent customer service is critical in the strategic planning of banks today. In order for customer service goals to be accomplished, every bank employee must become acutely aware of the needs and wants of both internal and external customers and must develop the skills and habits that make excellent customer service "the way we do things around here." This training program is designed to translate these identified goals into reality.

Definition of the Customer: A Conceptual Overview

Typically, the customer in the banking industry has been defined as the person who walks in the door to utilize the financial services offered. Certainly, this person's experiences with the bank are critical, for these experiences form the "moments of truth" that lead to the customer's perceptions and resultant future choices about the use of services.

However, there is another very important type of customer that impacts the overall service delivery—the internal customer. These customers are fellow employees, supervisors, and supervisees with whom clear communication, understanding, negotiation, and conflict resolution are necessary if the atmosphere and efficiency of the bank are to be positive. It has been said that employees will only treat customers as well as they are treated. One has only to recall the difficulty in being pleasant and attentive while being preoccupied with anger and resentment to affirm the truth of this statement.

Thus, the training program must address the concepts and skills needed to attend to the needs of both internal and external customers. Further, each individual must learn the personal adaptation and coping skills needed to turn problems into positive opportunities. It is to these ends that the following training program is designed. [See Figure 6-2.]

Figure 6-2
Training Program Outline

SUPERVISORY TRAINING

The critical role of managers and supervisors in the customer service program cannot be overemphasized. No matter how well-trained the front-line work force, the program will fail if supervisors do not competently and consistently model, reinforce, and reward excellent customer service. Supervisors will learn all skills taught to employees, as well as skills in positive performance management and appraisal. A session-by-session outline is presented below.

Session 1: A. Customer Service: An Overview
            B. Supervisor as Coach
            C. Leadership Styles
Session 2: A. Personal Reactions in an Environment of Change
            B. The Value of Team Building
            C. Building and Motivating the Team
Session 3: A. Essentials of Clear Communication
            B. One-Way vs. Two-Way Communication
            C. Active Listening Skills
Session 4: A. Identifying Personality and Communication Styles of Self and Others
            B. Feedback: How Am I Perceived by Others?
            C. Blending and Capitalizing on Differences
Session 5: A. Sources of Conflict in the Workplace
            B. Win-Win Negotiations
            C. Conflict Resolution Skills
Session 6: A. Moments of Truth: Raising Awareness
            B. Customer Service: Goals and Standards

Figure 6-2
Training Program Outline *continued*

Session 7: A. Building Rapport with the External Customer
              B. Responding and Relating to the Customer
              C. Customer Conflicts
Session 8: A. Performance Management: An Overview
              B. Planning and Goal Setting
              C. Behavior Observation
Session 9: A. Feedback Skills
                    1. Positive Feedback
                    2. Negative Feedback
              B. Introduction to Performance Problem Discussions
Session 10: A. Performance Problem Discussion: Demonstration and Practice
              B. Disciplinary Discussions
              C. Documentation
Session 11: A. Myths about Performance Appraisal
              B. How to Avoid Rating Errors
              C. Preparation for the Performance Appraisal
              D. Procedure for Performance Appraisal
Session 12: A. Performance Appraisal Practice
              B. Dealing with Difficult Employee Reactions
              C. Action Planning

EMPLOYEE TRAINING

Session 1: A. Customer Service: An Overview
              B. The Value of Teambuilding
              C. Personal Reactions in an Environment of Change
Session 2: A. Essentials of Clear Communication
              B. One-Way vs. Two-Way Communication
              C. Active Listening Skills
Session 3: A. Identifying Personality and Communication Styles of Self and Others
              B. Feedback: How Am I Perceived by Others?
              C. Blending and Capitalizing on Differences
Session 4: A. Sources of Conflict in the Workplace
              B. Win-Win Negotiations
              C. Conflict Resolution Skills
Session 5: A. Responding to Different Styles of Leadership
              B. Moments of Truth: Raising Awareness
              C. Customer Service: Setting Personal Goals

Figure 6-2
Training Program Outline *continued*

Session 6: A. Building Rapport with the Customer B. Communication with the Customer C. Adapting to the Customer's Preferred Communication Style D. Psychological Needs of the Customer Session 7: A. Responding and Relating to the Customer B. Reasons Customers Complain C. Responding to Customer Complaints D. Dealing with Several Customers at the Same Time E. Transferring and Referring Customers F. Handling Criticism Session 8: A. Dealing with Customer Conflicts B. Potential Conflict Situations C. Controlling Your Own Anger With a Customer D. How to "Cool Off" an Angry Customer E. Some "Sure-Fire" Ways to Make a Customer Angry F. Summary and Action Planning
FORMAT   Each session will be 3-1/2 hours in length. Content focus is on real-world behavior; that is, on doing something more often and more effectively in the "real world." It is highly recommended that both trainers be utilized in the supervisory training sessions in order to maximize exposure of participants to the contributions of each, resulting in greater knowledge acquisition and skill development. One trainer will then be consistently responsible for teaching two groups of employees (four groups in all).
Used with the permission of Dr. Beverly Sandifer-Smallwood, President of Smallwood Associates.

Results of the Survey

What benefits did the participants take away from the sessions? Post-training evaluations showed that a strong sense of teamwork and family was replacing the atmosphere of mistrust and infighting that had characterized the culture of the bank. One teller said the following when asked to respond to the changes that she has experienced in her relationship to other employees and customers:

> I am becoming a better listener. I can communicate better with coworkers. I am treating customers as if they are the most important people in the world, regardless of the transaction.

Other employees said the following:

> I am more willing to share my ideas for improving the efficiency and effectiveness of our organization. The feeling is that management is more receptive to ideas for positive change. Already we have enacted procedures to help insure loan compliance more fully and more efficiently than before.

> I have begun to focus even more on the customer. I have begun to go out of my way to greet customers and help them with a problem myself if I can, rather than just taking the customer somewhere else because "it's not my department."

One employee reported seeing the relationship between employee morale and customer service more clearly:

> I feel very good about the bank. The bank has been through a lot of changes in the last few years. The administration seems to be concerned with the employees' happiness and their feelings. When the employees are happy with their workplace, it carries over to their work. They are more loyal to the bank and more active in ideas that the bank wants carried out. This feeling of happiness carries over to the customer, which makes for a happier, more satisfied customer.

How did the employees feel about the training? Two employees stated the following:

> Personally I know this program was geared for customer service, but I know a lot more came out of it than customer service. I think we had internal problems that needed working on. These are things that reflected on customer service.

Working on those things has enabled us to give a much higher level of service.

These training programs have helped us move the bank in a real positive direction. The atmosphere in the bank is one of caring, courtesy; it's a warm and friendly place. This is something that the customers readily pick up on.

Norquist and the rest of senior management understood the halo effect from the training and were further aware that in order for this sense of teamwork and cooperation to continue, they must actively support it. That is why all senior management participated in the entire training program, *not just the 36 hours for the supervisors or the 24 hours for the employees but the entire 60 hours of training!*

What impression did this make on the employees? The basic opinion of employees was, "If you don't have the CEO's commitment to the training effort, you don't have everyone's commitment."

Van Ray, Senior Vice President, echoed this sentiment:

When the employees saw senior management sitting next to them in the training sessions, they realized that we were serious about the training. During this training they began to realize how dependent we were upon the customer.

One of the tellers remarked:

When I saw Griffin [Norquist] and Van [Ray] in the training sessions, I knew that everything that they had been saying about customer service was really important. I was so glad to see that this was not something that they were just talking about but was really important.

What does Norquist advise other CEOs regarding their involvement in customer service training?

They have got to do it! They cannot delegate! They have to take part in every aspect of it. That's the only way it gets credence. Each senior management person and also supervisors gave up 60 hours of his or her time sitting in training sessions. If you're not willing to put in this time, it won't work.

Not all is peaches and cream at the BYC, however. Several employees indicated that there were still problems. One employee stated, "I still see problems and it really discourages me, especially when you think of all the time and effort that we have put into the training. A number of us are waiting to see if these problems do get dealt with."

Norquist and his senior management team are aware of the need to assure both management and employees that their move to customer service is not just another "flavor of the month" and that they are in it for the long haul. This is a definite concern of Norquist. He explained:

> One of the major reservations that the staff had was that this was a passing fad. This was also a major reservation of the management staff. And that has been something that we have constantly had to reassure them about. We are in it for the long run. If the person who is directing the customer service effort leaves, we will designate someone else to carry on. You have to give it that commitment.

Norquist is a realist when it comes to the effects of training programs. He is not so naive as to believe that a couple hours of training will turn his bank into the top customer service option in the market. What does he see as the real benefits of this type of training?

> I think that the incredible thing to me is that I wouldn't say anyone is so much happier with their job. After all, who is really happy about a job? But I think that there is a comfort in most areas. There are still some interpersonal problems and we will always have these types of problems. But I think they are more comfortable dealing with each other and the customer. Heretofore, there was a sense that in dealing with the customer you had to win the argument. Winning was important. *Now the important thing is making sure that the customer is treated well and if a problem has occurred, that problem is solved.*

Rolling Out the Customer Service Carpet

Once Norquist felt that the BYC was capable of delivering on its claims of customer service, it was time to introduce the "new and improved BYC" to the public. Norquist commissioned his ad agency, which had been on-board with the strategy change since the formulation of the strategic statement, to develop a brochure and other promotional items that would announce the high quality of customer service that was available at the BYC.

Previously, the BYC had been advertising around a basic proposition "IT'S YOUR BANK." The new campaign continued this theme of ownership with a slight twist. Instead of continuing to claim that it was the customer's bank, the BYC proclaimed, "IT'S OUR BANK, TOO." The idea behind this approach was that all 34 employees of the BYC were proud of the bank and the changes that the bank had made over the past year. Figure 6-3 is a copy of the brochure centered around the new campaign.

Several aspects of this brochure merit additional attention, especially as they relate to the BYC philosophy of customer service. The first is the idea of the guarantee. Norquist argued, "Everyone guarantees good service but not many people back it up. We have gone a step further. I have personally signed my name to a pledge that we will provide our customers with the highest quality of customer service available in this market."

Not only did he sign his name to this pledge, but he also backed up the guarantee with a promise. The promise is the following:

> **If you ever become dissatisfied with our service in any way, we'll not only fix the problem, we'll also give you a choice of one of the following:**

- $10 credit to your account

- 1/2% interest off a new installment loan

Figure 6–3
It's Our Bank, Too!

It's our
bank, too!

"At Bank of Yazoo City, we're committed to quality, value and customer service."

Griffin Norquist

Griffin Norquist, Jr.
President
Bank of Yazoo City

III
BANK OF
YAZOO CITY
FOUNDED 1876 • MEMBER FDIC

Bank of Yazoo City has always based its business philosophy on a strong commitment to customer service. Now, we've gone a step further and formalized that commitment along with a promise to our customers:

If you ever become dissatisfied with our service in any way, we'll not only fix the problem, we'll also give you a choice of one of the following:

- $10 credit to your account
- 1/2% interest off a new installment loan
- No service charge on checking for three months

- Free use of safe deposit box for one year
- No annual fee on Visa/MasterCard for one year.

And, we're so sure that you'll be happy with Bank of Yazoo City that we'll make you another offer:

If you move your account to Bank of Yazoo City and are not satisfied, we'll personally move your account back to your previous bank at no cost to you.

We like to think we're taking care of people rather than just taking care of business.

Bank of Yazoo City prides itself on the high level of customer service we offer. It's our people who make the difference; we value each and every customer as an individual. You'll find the names and home phone numbers of persons whom you can contact with a problem. We're available when you need us; any time, day or night.

We promise quality, value, dedication to service, and guaranteed customer satisfaction. *That's* why we're proud to say, "It's *our* bank." We want to be your bank, too.

Griffin Norquist, Jr.
President.................. home 746-1898
office 746-5421, ext. 23
Robert Bailey
Executive
Vice President..........home 746-5398
office 746-5421, ext. 22
Joe Bryan
Vice President..........home 746-7099
office 746-5421, ext. 37
Van Ray
Vice President..........home 746-9099
office 746-5421, ext. 21
Carolyn Bryan
Vice President......... home 746-7099
office 746-5421, ext. 42

III
BANK OF
YAZOO CITY
FOUNDED 1876 • MEMBER FDIC

- No service charge on checking for 3 months

- Free use of a safe deposit box for one year

- No annual fee on Visa/Master Card for one year

Norquist also added one final kicker to this guarantee:

If you move your account to Bank of Yazoo City and are not satisfied, we'll personally move your account back to your previous bank at no cost to you.

To sock home the idea of commitment that Norquist feels is such an integral part of the BYC approach, he has put the home telephone numbers of the management team in the brochure. If any customer has a problem he or she can have immediate access to one of the top management at any time of the day. The idea here is that if a problem occurs, Norquist wants that problem dealt with immediately. The speed and the degree of recovery from an initial problem will have a strong bearing on whether that individual stays a customer of BYC or whether that individual will go elsewhere.

Developing a Set of Standards

In addition to the new campaign, Betty Nickels, the Director of Marketing at BYC, developed a set of standards for the appearance of the facility, teller skills, and platform sales rep skills. For the tellers, these standards will include such items as:

Noncustomer activity. This includes what the teller does at the window when there are customers waiting to be served and how the teller handles the customer while performing these other duties.

Waiting time to be served by a teller. Specific time standards will be developed governing the maximum amount of waiting time customers will have to endure.

Interpersonal skills. This includes how a teller initiates a service encounter; how the teller handles the transaction; how the teller closes the transaction; and the professional appearance of the teller.

Standards for the platform personnel have also been developed. They include the following:

Interpersonal dealings. Included in this group of standards are such items as noncustomer activity and how the customer is handled during the performance of other duties; the use of the customer's name; communication skills that include the degree of eye contact, smile, demonstration of concern and interest; professional appearance; and the use of the customer's name in closing.

Inquiry and problem solving skills. This includes the perception that the customer has that the platform rep really understands the customer's problem; how well the customer believes that the problem has been taken care of; the accuracy of the transaction; and the timeliness of the response.

Selling skills. Selling skills encompass such capabilities as listening; the ability to ask questions that more clearly define customer needs; product knowledge as demonstrated by the ability to fit bank services to customer needs; the ability to handle customer objections; the ability to close a sale; the follow up; and the use of sales aids.

These various standards form the basis of continual training programs for the bank employees. In addition, to insure compliance and to assess overall service delivery, the BYC is contemplating the use of customers as shoppers to shop the service level that they are offering. Currently, Norquist has been using a focus group format to both understand what customers want as well as to assess the current ability of the BYC to deliver quality service.

Is it Working?

This is one of the most frequent questions asked about the use of customer service as a strategic option. There are several answers to this question. The first answer focuses on the attitudes and the behavior of the employees at BYC. One of the principal objectives of the strategy was to instill pride in the employees and to build a more cohesive team at the BYC. Does it work? Ask any employee as we did and they will tell you about how proud they are of the bank and their fellow employees. For the most part, the feelings of mistrust and infighting that had pervaded the bank have been replaced with a new *esprit de corps*.

Do the customers notice the change in the way that business is done at BYC? Several comments from customers indicate that the atmosphere of BYC has changed to a more "caring, courteous, warm, and friendly place." Moreover, this new found sense of pride has shown up in the way the bank addresses its community involvement. Norquist told a story about BYC's participation in the local March of Dimes Walkathon. "Most banks had two to six people participating. We had over 60, including our spouses." Norquist called it, "almost embarrassing to see how BYC people dominated the walkathon." The interesting thing about the remarkable turnout, as Norquist was quick to point out, was that, "The staff did it all on their own."

Individual examples of customer service abound. Joe Bryan, a Senior Vice President who handles agricultural loans, is one of the service heroes at BYC. About a year ago, ten cotton growers had gotten together to pick one last field. Until then it hadn't rained at all, although rain was predicted some time after midnight. Norquist related the following story:

> Joe went down there to see if they were going to make it. The farmer, whose field they were picking, was not one of our customers. They were pulling cotton trailers but they ran out of trucks. So Joe hooked his truck up to a trailer and helped pull trailers until well after midnight. This is not just a one-time occurrence. One of the farmers turned to another and said, "I bet your loan officer doesn't help you harvest your cotton, does he?"

This is another indication of the basic customer service philosophy at the BYC. If you serve the customer first, the banking business will take care of itself.

Norquist was quick to point out that the customer service strategy is working in other ways as well. A quality circle solved a problem that has saved the bank a significant amount of money. Ray explained:

> We were bringing the branch people in at seven in the morning. They were trying to handle the previous day's work before nine, when they were scheduled to be opened. They modified the internal control of the handling of night deposit

bags to speed up the process. They saved the bank some money. We no longer had to pay them for the extra two hours of work and the employees were happy they didn't have to come in so early.

Finally, how has the customer service strategy affected the bottom line of the bank? Employees in the bank report a higher degree of customer activity. Bank management is in the process of tracking new accounts and loans and relating them to the change in strategic direction. An initial reading of financial changes suggests that the BYC is already seeing positive signs of their strategic shift. Since 1988, BYC has increased its deposit base from $70.5 million to over $77 million. Projections for 1993 peg deposits at over $89 million. During this same period (88-90) ROA has edged up from a solid 1.00 to 1.06.

Tips from the Top

What advice does Norquist offer to those who are contemplating a customer service strategy? Norquist is adamant about the need for commitment on the part of top management. A customer service strategy will not work unless top management is behind it all the way.

This is something that we have seen in our work with other banks. It is not uncommon to find the words "customer service" listed in a bank's mission statement or printed on advertising or bandied about the board room. *However, it is much more difficult to find a bank that has taken the idea of customer service and all that it entails and made it a working reality.*

Norquist's commitment and that of his senior staff is evidenced in their participation in the training programs that all employees attended. A lack of CEO commitment is common in banks that merely claim to employ a customer service strategy, instead of deliver it. "You cannot delegate," Norquist said. "The CEO has to take part in every aspect of the strategy implementation. That's the only way it gets credence. If he or she is not willing to do it, I wouldn't even try it."

"A second key to success is that you have to treat employees as you would a customer," explained Norquist. A basic belief on the part of the BYC management is that there is a direct correlation between the way people treat each other in the bank and the way they treat customers. Norquist and his management have spent a lot of time improving the culture of the bank. The initial thrust of the strategy implementation was creating the teamwork and the sense of worth that individuals feel toward the organization. Employee turnover has averaged about 1% over the last five years. A sense of pride pervades the Bank of Yazoo City. Employees talk about "going one step beyond in serving the customer" and proudly proclaim that, "there is not another bank in the area that gives the quality of service that we do." At the bottom of this service culture is the idea voiced by one employee, "Service quality and the customer mean a lot to me!"

Perhaps the most important point, in Norquist's opinion, is the need for the CEO to give up control. By giving up control Norquist means *"emotional control."* In effect, Norquist is suggesting that the president has to give up some power in decision making. "You have to have confidence in your staff." When asked how you can tell when the staff has the capability to assume a greater responsibility in the conduct of the bank, Norquist responded, "It's a trial and error process. You make mistakes but you learn from them."

Norquist has, in essence, turned the BYC organizational chart upside down. At the top of the chart is the customer and the staff. Lower down is middle management, followed by senior management and then the CEO. Accompanying this structural change is an open communication system which guarantees that employees are heard. This shift in focus has been tough for Norquist. The first time he was confronted by an employee suggestion, he responded, "Absolutely not. I'm not going to do that. Then I calmed down and listened to what they were saying and found out that they were right. The suggestion addressed something that I had done wrong. I was still reacting to emotional control." Norquist readily admits that the people who are serving the customer on a daily basis are doing something, "that is much more important than what I do."

Another reason why the change to a customer service strategy is working so well at the BYC is that, while Norquist might be hesitant to talk about his own behavior as CEO, it is obvious that he is highly respected within the bank and acts as a role model to other bank employees. His management style is very open and has been characterized by several employees as, "If I'm in trouble, Griffin is right there for me." He has, in part, by the force of his own personality, created an environment that is conducive to providing the level of service that is necessary to make BYC the top bank in the area. Employees see Norquist as a role model, one who is always going the extra mile to help a customer. He is often described as a coach by employees, offering advice and help to anyone who needs it. That is not to say that he doesn't criticize. He will and does. But the interesting thing is that employees who receive the criticism respond to it positively. Customer service has become a way of life at the Bank of Yazoo City as a result.

Customer Service a la the Community Bank

A smaller community bank offers both opportunities and problems in instituting a strong emphasis on customer service. The down side may be the amount of money available to invest in the development and implementation of the strategy. However, this is offset by the smallness of the bank and its ability to provide more attentive service, which may prove to be its most important and significant asset.

Developing a service culture in a small single office or a main bank with one branch is easier than changing the culture in a bank with numerous branch locations. Moreover, as Ray has pointed out, a customer service strategy offers the community bank an opportunity to dictate the terms of competition in a local market area instead of having to try and follow a larger leader institution. Their size can lead to a proficiency that becomes a standard for service delivery in the market area.

Because of the size of the community bank, relative to larger multiple branch banks for example, the role of the CEO in the formulation and implementation of the strategy will more than likely be different. The CEO may need to become more of a *leader* as opposed to a *manager.* His or her actions speak very loudly in the smaller setting. This is seen by the impact that the presence of Norquist and Ray and other senior officers had on employees during the training sessions. In fact, Norquist is extremely adamant regarding the participation of the CEO in the implementation of the strategy. Norquist is a leader at BYC and his actions set examples for the rest of the employees.

While it is often typical to measure commitment in terms of dollars spent, commitment can also be measured in terms of the time top management is willing to devote to turning the organization into a quality customer service leader. This is the case at BYC. While the cost of the development and implementation of the customer service strategy may pale in comparison to the actual dollar cost incurred at much larger banks, the *time* top management has spent is indicative of their commitment to a higher quality service delivery system.

The Bank of Yazoo City demonstrated the importance of breaking the cyclical relationship between poor employee morale and poor customer service. This was one of the first problems addressed at BYC. Once a sense of teamwork was seeded into the culture and employees began cooperating with each other, it was possible to focus energy and attention on the customer. Both customer and employee comments support the importance of employee satisfaction with their jobs in the delivery of high quality customer service.

Chapter

Customer Service at Concord Commercial Bank

The Setting

Concord Commercial Bank is located in the center of Concord, California, the largest city within Contra Costa County, approximately twenty-six miles east of San Francisco. The 1980s saw significant growth in the city's population from 103,000 in 1980 to approximately 112,000 in 1990 with projections for a 10% population growth from 1990 to 2005. Manufacturing and wholesale jobs employment are expected to grow nearly 43% during the 1990-2005 period with retail jobs increasing over 27%.

The Concord Chamber of Commerce describes the city as follows:

> With its convenient location, skilled workforce, and highly competitive development costs, Concord is now home to some of the nations's most prominent businesses, becoming one of

the Bay Area's leading commercial business centers. Concord's emphasis on economic development benefits both existing industry and prospective companies. The city maintains a professional economic development program headed by an experienced director and strong working relationships with the private sector through the Concord Chamber of Commerce, realtors, and developers. The private sector has been particularly aggressive and effective in Concord's developing prestigious office space, first quality manufacturing and warehousing facilities, and attractive and reasonable industrial parks and sites, complete with utilities and access roads.

The business climate in Concord is one which pays great respect to the free enterprise system and provides a solid foundation for fostering new businesses and generating the profits of existing businesses. Prospective industrialists and entrepreneurs can expect a stable and predictable fiscal environment including a local government which is tightly and responsibly managed.

Both the private and public sectors have been aggressive in developing attractive and sophisticated office and industrial parks so that companies surveying the region as a business location are pleased by the broad and diverse locational alternatives presented them. Concord prides itself on its unwavering support for a positive business climate and looks forward to becoming home to an ever growing number of corporations from around the world.

Tom Hawker, Chief Executive Officer at Concord Commercial Bank (CCB), described the development of the bank as follows: "Concord Commercial Bank was formed in 1985 by a group of business people from the Concord area who had become disenchanted with their banking relationships at Wells Fargo, Bank of America, Security Pacific, and other large Bay area banks." Hawker pointed out that while there was nothing inherently bad about these banks, their strategies did not mesh well with the need of a small- to medium-sized business in the Bay area. The feeling of disenchantment came not because of bad service in a generic context but rather as a result of a poor matching of bank capabilities and customer needs within a more narrowly-defined market. It was the perception of these small- to medium-sized business people that the large Bay area banks were seeking primarily to serve large commercial clients and were, therefore, seeking volume related economies. The large banks were looking for large loans and large deposits where volume would drive higher profits from lower margins. This created *transactional* banking relationships with smaller customers and was not a satisfactory relationship for business people seeking more personal and individual service. This transactional approach to banking resulted in the market segment experiencing lower levels of service than they felt they deserved, and, in fact, demanded.

A point should be reinforced here. It is not improper for a large bank to pursue a strategy of transactional banking where profits are enhanced by volume rather than individual service. However, this strategy is not suited for every market segment and opportunities for other strategic deliveries of service exist when market segments expand to the point where they are large enough and prosperous enough to support a bank offering a demanded alternative. This is exactly what the founders and organizers of CCB recognized and which CCB is based upon. They perceived the inability or unwillingness of large banks to reconfigure their operations and approach to small- to medium-sized businesses to provide a higher quality of individualized service. So, an opportunity was recognized and a group was brought together to form a bank in their own image—Concord Commercial Bank.

Concord Commercial Bank, CCB, was formed on the premise of individualized and personal service to the small- to medium-sized business in the Concord/Contra Costa area. This was the single focus of CCB at inception, and it continues to be so today. Hawker emphatically stated that CCB exists solely to serve the image of the bank organizers and seeks to do little else. In fact, CCB remains so true to its basic purpose that individual accounts are not accepted without a corresponding commercial account relationship. Customers seeking an individual account relationship without a commercial relationship are literally referred across the street—one direction to Bank of America and the other direction to Wells Fargo. We will have more to say about this strict focus in a later section when we talk about implementation of CCB's strategy.

The close of the year of 1985, the first year of CCB's operation saw total assets at nearly $15,000,000, total deposits $10,200,000, total loans of $6,800,000 and a net loss of $445,000, certainly not unexpected for the first year of operation. However, 1986 was indicative of the future of CCB. At close of business in 1986, total assets had grown 66% to nearly $25,000,000; total deposits increased 98% to $20,100,000, total loans grew 146% to $16,700,000 and net loss for the year decreased by 69% to a net loss of $138,000. The second year of operation was truly remarkable.

From the end of 1985 through the third quarter of 1989, total assets had grown 207% to nearly $46,000,000; total deposits increased 295% to over $40,000,000; total loans grew to $34,300,000, a 405% increase and net income grew to $588,000, annualized for 1989.

What explains this phenomenal growth rate and performance for CCB? Hawker offered one external explanation:

> A sister community, Walnut Creek, some seven years ago (around 1983), had a city council which initiated a no-growth policy for its city. By this, they sent a discouraging message relative to business entry, growth, and expansion. Concord, however, had a very progressive city government and actively encouraged business growth and expansion. So, CCB was well positioned, having organized some two years after Walnut Creek's no-growth policy, to capitalize on somewhat a disproportionate way on the business climate created at the time.

> And as one can see, CCB somewhat mirrors the growth of Concord. Examining the taxable retail sales of Concord from 1985 through 1988 one observes an increase of nearly 51%. This is compared to deposits of CCB increasing 276% during

the same period. So, CCB did more that just mirror the city's growth and performance, it far exceeded it to the extent that retail sales can be directly compared to deposits.

Not only were we successful with our timing, but we are also firmly and narrowly focused on our strategy for our market— something the other banks were not. So we like to believe that our external circumstances were aided by our implementation of a focused strategy that accounts for our performance over the past five years.

The Concord Strategy

Now that the context in which CCB conducts banking business has been explained, it is important to examine what CCB tells customers, employees, and the public about the bank. The following sections taken from CCB's annual reports discuss their strategy:

The purpose of Concord Commercial Bank is to:
- Provide an attractive long-term return to our shareholders' investment.
- Provide everyone associated with us an efficient and enjoyable banking experience.

Through our "Business and Bank...Growing Together" approach, our officers and staff constantly strive to earn your customers' continued confidence.

The Mission Statement of Concord Commercial Bank is to:
- Provide every customer with personal, efficient, and professional banking services designed to meet the financial needs of the business and professional firms located in our service area.
- Consistently strive for a return for our investors that exceeds banking industry standards.
- Provide a rewarding and stimulating work environment for our employees.

- Contribute our time, talents, and monies to the goal of making our communities a better place in which to live and work.

Concord Commercial Bank's mission will be successful by:
- Maintaining a reputation as a financial institution where it is a pleasure to do business, to invest, and to work.
- Achieving above average growth without sacrificing quality, service, or profitability.
- Aggressively pursuing and retaining high quality relationships.
- Earning a position of respect as an organization that is a responsible member of the community.

Purpose and Mission Statements

One of the initial objectives in CCB's purpose and mission statements is the recognition of the long-term return to shareholders. This is consistent with the investment in building long lasting relationships with business customers. Secondly is the purpose of providing enjoyable banking experiences to customers and employees as well. The aspect of providing an enjoyable banking experience is an interesting one in light of our book *Winning Banks*. In our research for *Winning Banks*, we found that customers typically describe their banking experiences in rather dry, mundane, task-oriented terms—just something to be endured but not enjoyed, like mopping the kitchen floor. But, CCB is interested in altering the typical experience to one in which the customer looks forward to it and actually gets some satisfaction from their banking relationship. This necessarily implies that personal and individualized attention exist.

The next striking part of CCB's purpose statement is the designation of its strategy—"Business and Banking...Growing Together." This clearly designates CCB as a business bank and is communicated to customers, employees, investors, and all others reading its literature. This statement appears in annual reports, quarterly statements, newspaper ads, and nearly all correspondence originating from the bank. "Business and Banking...Growing

Together" represents in five simple words what CCB is and what it intends to do.

The mission statement provides further refinement and expansion of the purpose of CCB. For example, the personal and individualized service given in the bank is expressly provided for in the mission statement. In addition, the mission statement defines its criteria for success as maintaining a good reputation, growing without sacrificing quality, pursuing high quality relationships, and being a good corporate citizen.

Customer Service the Concord Way

The purpose and mission statements of CCB seem remarkably similar to many other banks across the country. For example, the words efficient, confidence, professional, personal, and quality are commonly found in the statement of purpose and mission of many banks. No banks say they want to be inefficient, unconfident, unprofessional, impersonal, and provide poor quality of service. But how is it that CCB puts action behind these positive attributes and makes them more than empty words? What does CCB do that sets them apart from other banks in the Bay area? The following are some points that separate CCB from others and are the subject of interviews with Hawker and his staff.

An Open Management Philosophy—Employee Meetings

When we entered the lobby of CCB one Thursday morning around 8:15 AM, we were made part of a weekly event at CCB—an employee meeting led by Tom Hawker. This is a good place to begin an explanation of what is meant by "Customer Service the Concord Way." Hawker considers this meeting time to be a forum for the exchange of information to be shared by *all* the employees of the bank concerning subjects from earnings to a description and discussion of new customers and their businesses. There are two impressive aspects of this approach. First, there doesn't appear to be a subject with which Hawker chooses not to openly discuss. Our impression is that Hawker covers it all to inform employees just how the bank is performing—both good and bad. Secondly, Hawker talked about new customers. Not only did he receive a new accounts report detailing numbers of accounts and dollars, he compiled a report on names and descriptions of new customers of the bank so that when a customer called or came by, he or she would be known. Hawker explained: "This tells everyone about new customers. It is important to us that if a new name pops up at the teller window that someone recognize it and say something."

Hawker offered the following story to suggest how this effort pays off for CCB:

> We had a father and son come into our bank with the same name, except for Jr. and Sr. In addition, the father's wife and daughter-in-law had the same name. We spent quite some time in our regular weekly meeting telling our employees that there was a Jr. and Sr. with quite different net worth and credit history and not to mess up.

This distinction is important to CCB employees because they offer personal, individualized service. If they offer good quality and personal service they cannot afford to confuse a Jr. and a Sr. To do so invalidates their promise of service on a personal basis. So, CCB spends time to ensure that a mess-up never happens.

Hawker continued with another service quality story:

> A lady whose husband had just opened an account with CCB came into our bank. One of our account representatives recognized her name and started helping her. Then someone else came over to her and said, "I understand you and your husband are banking with us now." Well, she went home and told her husband about this experience. Her husband called me the next morning and told me how his wife appreciated this banking experience so much that she opened three new accounts. I wish I could say it happened every day, but this is what we encourage to happen by informing our whole staff about our customers and their businesses.

This shared knowledge of customers also involves telephone contact as well as face-to-face contact. Hawker explained:

> Since the day this bank opened, telephone etiquette has been important. When a customer calls into the bank, no matter who answers the phone, the likelihood is good that the employee will recognize the customer's name and will make the customer aware of this.

This policy is a direct result of informing employees in an open meeting about customers of the bank. Hawker initiated a firm policy in the bank that the phone rings a maximum of twice before it is answered. On the day we were at CCB, the phone usually rang only once before it was answered. Although CCB has a person primarily responsible for answering the phone, *everyone* in the bank is attuned to the two-ring rule and everyone will answer it—no matter what their primary job is! This includes Hawker as well. Hawker explained:

> I make it a practice to personally answer the phone two or three times a day. It helps me keep a feel for who is calling and their needs, but it also demonstrates to the staff that no one in this bank is too important to answer the phone. I do it and they see me. This communicates better than a memo or verbal instructions. I set the example.

This point is repeated time and time again throughout the bank. Hawker leads his staff by example!

Another planned benefit of weekly employee meetings is Hawker's philosophy of multiple contacts for the customer. The employee meeting enables employees to share information so that more than one CCB employee can effectively serve the customer. Service continues uninterrupted even when someone is out of the bank. This is an important aspect of CCB's quality of service. The customer must know that CCB works closely as a team to serve them and help them. Even when one team member is unavailable, the other team members will take up the slack so the customer is served well. Hawker explained:

> If I am not here, it does not interrupt anything. This is a matter of empowering staff and informing customers. We try not to make customer relationships just one on one, but we try to have multiple contacts within the bank. I have only a few customers because I cannot do all of what is expected from me and service all customers well. My staff must be empowered to make decisions on behalf of customers. I am not going to make all the decisions and I want our customers to recognize that our officers and employees are going to make decisions.

Physical Layout of CCB

One of the most striking features of the physical layout of CCB is the sign on its front door. The sign reads, "Banking Hours—9 AM - 4 PM *Other Hours by Appointment*." Yes! Other hours are available to customers of CCB simply by calling and arranging for an appointment. Hawker explained:

> There is usually someone in CCB at 7:30 AM until 6:30-7:00 PM. every business day. If a customer calls, we will let them in and do business. Or, as is the case many times, if a customer is recognized at the door, we will open the door and welcome them in. We will be here when the customer wants to do business.

This feeling was echoed many times in interviews with other employees. Employee, Shelia Pugh, said that employees will stay as long as it takes to serve the customer. Apparently Hawker has been quite successful in communicating the need to be available when the customer wants service. Most people are accustomed to seeing heavy draperies pulled across the doors and windows of the bank at closing time—almost a symbol of blocking out the customer. Hawker added, "As long as there is someone that can provide service, we want to do it. One of the luxuries of having fewer customers is if someone calls or comes to the door, generally you know who it is. But, fewer customers is by design and entirely consistent with our strategy—focus on commercial accounts."

Other physical attributes of CCB were also related to providing quality service. For example, there are no traditional teller windows. This deviation from traditional bank design took place at the inception of the bank and is indicative again of CCB's management philosophy. Hawker explained:

> This design represents an idea and an attitude. We are not looking for quantity, but rather we are looking for quality. We are looking to do *relationship banking* instead of *transactional banking* and that means we want to spend more time dealing with the individual customer rather than having lots of people coming through the lobby. We do not want someone with a stopwatch in the lobby saying the service standard is fifty-three seconds and you took fifty-four seconds—you have to do better. That is why we have the sit-down windows with tellers at a desk. The idea is to make the customer feel like he or she is conducting business, instead of just processing a transaction. It is not a cattle chute approach to things, with no roped area feeding customers into teller windows.
>
> This approach has been very well received by our customers. They tell us they are much more comfortable handling their business and that is what we want—a comfortable and enjoyable banking experience. This was a design feature incorporated into the bank from the very beginning by our organizers because that is the way they wanted to do their business.

A quick trip through local competing bank branches located on opposite corners from CCB revealed roped-off areas through which customers flowed to a traditional teller window. In addition, each bank had a considerable line, from eight to twenty people, waiting to be served. A sign blinked the availability of the next teller position. What was interesting to note was that the available tellers were a considerable distance from the customer pooling area. This arrangement is hardly appropriate for the type of customer CCB serves; it is appropriate for transactional banking but not for relationship banking with personal, individualized service.

Another interesting point to note is that the teller lobby of CCB is rather small due to limited numbers of commercial customers. Therefore, when five customers are in the bank seeking teller service, the lobby gets full. Employees are attuned to this and will leave their office or desk to serve those customers who do not have cash needs. Even Hawker will step outside his office and take a check-only deposit rather than let a customer stand and wait for a teller. This is consistent with CCB's policy of referring individual accounts to another bank. With many individual customers come a crowded lobby, and a crowded lobby is something to be avoided as much as possible when serving commercial customers. According to Hawker, a crowded image is something CCB does not want.

Hawker also described some of the other physical attributes of CCB:

> One of the things I had to deal with was that our physical design was for a $20,000,000-$25,000,000 bank, not a $50,000,000 bank. With growth comes space limitations and problems. Our growth caused us to be more crowded than we like—so we acquired more space upstairs and made some changes to give us the needed space in the lobby. As it was, when three people were in the lobby it looked crowded and that was not the right perception. Interestingly, however, was that primarily support personnel were moved to the second floor with the customer contact personnel staying on the first floor to continue to be easily accessible to the customer.

With the second floor expansion, Hawker received encouragement to move his office off of the banking floor to free some of his time to perform his CEO duties. Hawker has some rather strong feelings about his office and location. He explained:

> I have observed over the years that as banks grow, the first thing the President or CEO wants to do is to get out of the middle of things. It is hard to get your job done with people coming in and out of your office all the time. But that is one of the reasons why people come into our bank—I am accessible and I am here for them to see me. Even if we just wave to each

other, there is a relationship that I cannot have with customers and they with me if I am upstairs out of the flow of business. This office will stay on the main banking floor where my customers are. I am committed to staying right here in the middle of the bank.

Another benefit that CCB has from having its CEO on the main banking floor is that the employees see him there as well. Tom Hawker leads by example. We observed this numerous times during the day; both Hawker and the employees greeted customers. He explained:

By my getting up and going out to talk to customers in the lobby it creates an example for everyone in the bank to follow. The message is no one is too important to get up from his or her desk and talk to customers.

Location of Concord Commercial Bank

As you approach Concord Commercial Bank near Town Square, you cannot help but notice its strategic location. It is situated between a branch of Wells Fargo and a branch of Bank of America. Literally, CCB is located in the middle of two of the largest banks in the Bay area and the U.S. The reason CCB is situated thusly is because of the original service philosophy of CCB and the reason the bank was organized. There was a strong feeling that the other large banks were not addressing the need of the small- and medium-sized businesses in the community. The other banks were looking for the large customer and the volume side of the business. The middle business market had become disenfranchised. The best place for CCB to be situated was between what its target markets perceived as its biggest banking problems—the other banks!

CCB is positioned where it is, both physically and strategically, as an alternative. The original CCB board determined the present location to be an excellent one. This site also happened to be the original location of Bank of America. In the recent memory of the people of Concord, this site was a banking location. In addition, the board was also committed to the revitalization of downtown Concord and wanted to be in the middle of it.

A central downtown location was not a disadvantage to CCB within its commercial market segment, due to the decision to run a daily courier service to pick up noncash deposits and deliver important documents to and from the bank. If the customer cannot come to the bank, the bank goes to the customer. Accessibility is fundamental to Concord's vision of customer service.

The Family of Concord

When discussing the personnel of CCB, one often hears the term "family" applied to the officers and employees. CCB's courier, Inga Blume, explained, "Everyone here is helpful to each other. This is a family type atmosphere—very cooperative. We help each other help our customers. Customers can tell how supportive we are of each other and how polite we are." This was a theme heard time and again from employees and customers as well. How does this sense of cooperative teamwork or family happen? It is a decided policy conceived and played out by the personality of Hawker and his supporting staff of officers.

The teamwork approach to managing a staff is also apparent in Hawker's personnel policies and procedures. Hiring is performed at the departmental level, but Hawker usually interviews all prospective employees as well. Here he discusses the importance of teamwork and fitting in with the Concord group of employees and customers. While final hiring decisions are made by department heads, Hawker has given the CCB quality of service message to each new employee.

There is no predetermined background to look for when hiring personnel. CCB does not require a prior banking background. Rebecca, the receptionist, was in fact, a beautician by trade. Blume, the courier, had no prior banking experience, but both fit well into CCB's way of doing business. Hawker explained:

> We hire people who like to deal with other people and are
> comfortable doing so. We will teach the team the mechanics of
> doing a job which is a relatively simple thing to teach. Mechanics
> is much easier to teach than relating well to others.

Wages are competitive at CCB but are no more nor less than at
other similar employment opportunities throughout the Bay area.
Therefore, pay is not used to attract a higher quality workforce.
Hawker, however, did provide stock options for his employees as
a way of creating ownership. His belief is that with ownership
comes increased feelings of responsibility for improvements in
service quality. In fact, Hawker believes very strongly in establishing ownership by the employees—ownership of their jobs,
their bank, and of their customer relationships. He says that
ownership is a combination of things such as 401(K) plans, social
functions, staff meetings, dress down days, picnics during the
summer, champagne after work when significant goals are passed,
and taking employees and spouses out to dinner at a restaurant of
their choice.

Another program to promote service quality is the Business
Partner of the Quarter. The Business Partner of the Quarter is
voted by the staff to recognize the employee who has done a good
job serving customers and fellow employees the prior quarter.
He or she is featured in news releases and other promotional
materials around Concord.

Hawker is also on a first name basis with employees because he
encouraged it. He explained that this helps promote teamwork and
he needs teamwork more than he needs to be called Mr. Hawker.

Another factor in quality service is the performance appraisal
process which basically occurs every six months on a formal
basis. There is an emphasis on quality service in the CCB
performance appraisal form. According to Hawker, "You must
measure it if you want someone to do it." However, with the
daily monitoring of service quality that exists in the bank by

Hawker and the other employees, something would probably be done to correct poor quality of service performance prior to a formal performance review.

Another personnel policy and procedure that exists within CCB, Hawker also originated. He had a stamp made that reads "From our Customers." He stamped this on all paychecks to officers and employees to remind everyone on a regular basis that their paycheck did not come from Tom Hawker, but rather from satisfied customers. This reinforces Hawker's belief that the way to keep customers, and, therefore, paychecks, was to give good quality service.

One of the striking features of Concord Commercial Bank, partly due to strategy and partly due to Hawker's philosophy of management, is the lack of formal management systems. Concord is run primarily as an informal system depending heavily on oral tradition to communicate the quality service ideal. We heard this time after time in interviewing employees and officers of Concord Bank. Comments like, "Service is an attitude at CCB" means that employees gain a sense of behavioral norms that include service quality. This attitude is built into the culture of CCB and is passed on informally by example. This example is reflected in the leadership role taken by Tom Hawker and then passed directly on to his staff who emulate his behavior toward customers. The bank is governed and the standards of service quality are established not by policy statements but rather by a committed staff who display the acceptable standard every day they show up at CCB to conduct business.

Bottom-lining the Concord Approach

There is no doubt that Tom Hawker and his staff do an outstanding job of delivering high quality customer service. When talking to customers about service quality in *Winning Banks*, we were constantly bombarded with horror stories of bad and uncaring service. Not so when we talked with Concord's customers. They all praised the level of service that they were getting from Hawker and his staff.

What we can learn from Concord is basically simple. First, Hawker is a customer service leader. He eats, sleeps, and sweats customer service and, in so doing, is a model for all Concord employees. It's hard to pin down Concord's secrets of customer service success. Their approach is empty of lists of standards, formalized incentive programs, exhaustive training programs, and massive volumes of strategic plans. Instead, when asked about their service delivery system, employees tell you, "It's the way we do business here" or "This is what Tom [Hawker] would do."

Hawker relies on creating an informal management system which strongly supports his strategy and personal desire to provide superior service. Hawker relies on being a role model for his employees and expects the employees to be role models for each other. He believes so strongly in providing the standard of behavior in his bank that he will not move his office off the main banking floor. This brings us to the conclusion that it is easier to be a CEO on the second floor but easier to be a leader on the main bank floor.

Another extremely important part of the customer service approach at Concord is that Hawker and his staff have an extremely focused strategy on a narrowly targeted market segment. They do not stray from this. Everything about this strategy pivots around the key concept of accessibility. Whether accessibility means being open WHEN the customers need the bank to be open, or whether it means being WHERE the customers need the bank to be with their courier service, or whether it means simply HOW the customer is served with their unique structural layout, Concord Commercial Bank provides accessibility.

Contrary to many other types of banks, Concord is run on a fairly informal basis. Much of the necessary communication is oral. Hawker runs an extremely open organization wherein all employees are given both information and the power to use that information to deliver the high quality service for which Concord Commercial is known. This works because there is a strong family culture in the bank. People help each other with the ultimate goal of providing the customer with outstanding service.

One of Hawker's biggest concerns is controlling the growth of the bank. Soon, he estimates, Concord Commercial will have to expand and when they do, maintaining the working environment and the culture of Concord will be his number one priority. He plans on doing this by seeding the new branch with current employees who can carry on the tradition of Concord and insure that service quality is the number one concern of all involved. Concord is strategically well-poised for success in the 1990s, able to compete very profitably with both current and potential institutions.

Chapter

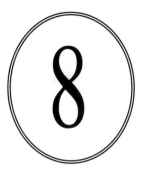

Customer Service as a Full Distribution Strategy at Seafirst Bank

Imagine going into a bank and asking for a checking account, a CD, a credit card, and a Big Mac with fries. Sound crazy? Not to Luke Helms, CEO of Seafirst Bank in Seattle, Washington. Helms envisions a franchise based banking system where individual branch managers not only run the "store" but buy their supplies and technical backup from a holding company. The sole purpose of the holding company is to establish location and develop and maintain image for the banking system. The job of the store owner is to sell and service banking clients. Moreover, Helms argues, if each store owner bought his or her franchise, imagine the dedication to customer service and profitability you would have.

Helms' vision may be atypical of what many bankers see as the natural evolutionary process of the industry. However, it really isn't that far removed from what Seafirst is attempting to do right now. To understand the way Seafirst Bank operates it is important to first understand how it got to be where it is today.

Get Good at Something, Quick!

According to Helms, the shift to the current strategy is traceable back to about 1982 or 1983. Seafirst lost a lot of money in the Penn Square situation forcing an earlier acquisition than many had anticipated. Seafirst was bought by Bank of America and given two basic directives. First, it was to focus only on the Pacific Northwest and second, it was to find something to be good at, quick. Helms explained:

> Actually, the series of events presented a unique opportunity to recreate the bank. Had we still been making a whole hell of a lot of money in 1982 or 1983, because we were always one of the more profitable banks in the U.S., year after year, through the 60s and 70s, we wouldn't have invested the money; we wouldn't have refocused. It's terribly expensive to sell customer service. It's really expensive.

Seafirst found itself presented with an opportunity to get out of a number of businesses in which it traditionally dealt. Losses in international banking and losses in national accounts outside of the Northwest where Seafirst did about 50% of their business forced Seafirst management to reconsider its current position. The ingredients were right to get into retail banking aggressively, but Helms explained, "The ingredients hit us earlier for all the wrong reasons." With a sound management team in place Seafirst was ready to redefine its mission and to develop a strategy for the future.

Seafirst's management team looked at several different strategies. Helms claimed, "We were too big to be a niche bank. In some areas we are a niche bank, but overall we're too big." A low cost strategy or what Helms called "a credit union or S&L look alike" was out of the question too. The only viable strategic alternative left was to become a retail bank. Helms explained:

You finally realize that you've got 150 to 200 stores out there and you're selling product and that you're not in the banking business, you're not in the niche business, you're not a low cost producer, you're a retailer! Then we all broke out in a cold sweat because we were all trained to be credit officers.

Market research provided some insight into how Seafirst needed to proceed. Research showed that banks, in general, were providing the consumer with what the consumer really did not want. While consumers wanted personal service, banks were responding with ATMs and other technology-driven products. In the face of a rapidly changing financial services industry, consumers wanted choice from their bank but were instead offered the same old traditional services and products.

Seafirst sent a number of people around the country to talk to the best retailers in America. A number of banks were included in this group of outstanding retailers. Once they were completed, Seafirst management went over their notes and came to the conclusion that none of the outstanding retailers were banks! Seafirst then went to the true retailers and began to get some ideas on how to turn a bank into a retail store. Nordstroms, a family-owned retail business headquartered in Seattle, consistently recognized as one of the outstanding deliverers of customer service in the United States, decorated one of the branches. They did more than just decorate it, however. Nordstroms explained how it should look, why it should look like it did, what the customer flows were, and how to design the inside so that it was friendly. "Our first strategy was to get into retail and be the best at it," said Helms.

The next step was a visit to McDonald's. "We spent, and continue to spend, an inordinate amount of time at McDonald's. I send a lot of people to Hamburger U. We are so impressed with their training we have a thing here called Seafirst College patterned in many ways like Hamburger U—How to Manage a Franchise," Helms said.

Helms described the Seafirst retail strategy as a three-legged stool. The three legs are: cost reduction, sales, and customer service. Seafirst initiated the following three-phased plan:

Phase One: Cost Reduction

The first leg of the stool was cost reduction. The overriding goal of this reduction was to pass the savings on to the customer. Cost reduction meant, in essence, working smarter. This was largely achieved through centralized processing.

Seafirst management took all of the processing out of the branches, thus allowing personnel to focus on sales and service. In 1984, Seafirst had 8,500 employees; today the number is 7,100. Reducing the number of employees was not easy for Seafirst management. They took advantage of normal employee attrition and turnover, but accelerated this reduction with early retirement programs. The reduction was not necessarily a permanent proposition—staffing needs are determined by customer needs, but are also subject to an eye on costs.

A key element in this cost-reduction move was the decision to centralize the paperwork and processing that each branch had handled independently in the past. This involved a significant investment in mainframe capabilities with the locating of user-friendly terminals throughout the system. A centralized operations group works with the branches and allows branch staff more time for sales and service. According to Marie Gunn, Senior Vice President and Manager of Quality Service, the cost reduction effort, "flattened down the organization and slashed staff areas. In essence we moved decision making back to the line functions."

The bottom line of this cost reduction move was to allow Seafirst to operate with about 20% less people resulting in a reduction of about 15% to 17% of its previous cost structure. A further aspect of this continuing focus on cost and concern for customer service is the philosophy of, "Do it right the first time." As Gunn said, "We feel that this is the point where cost and sales come together. If we do it right the first time, we reduce cost and provide great service!"

Phase Two: Developing a Sales Culture

It is in the installation of the sales culture at Seafirst where one really begins to notice Helm's vision of banking. Prior to deregulation Helms explained, "we operated in an era of tightly controlled product and pricing structures. The key to positioning a bank was the convenience of its branch locations." The key challenge now, according to Helms, was to enhance marketing through a strong proactive selling effort, a difficult task for an industry which did not necessarily equate banking with salesmanship.

One of the first steps was to establish a Personal Banker structure in the branch banks. Seafirst developed three tiers of personal banking, differentiated by the products and services it offered. Referring back to its market research, Seafirst also felt that there was a need to change its approach to customers. In other words, a hard selling approach had to be balanced by an ability to offer the customer constructive and solid financial advice. This called for an entirely new orientation to training.

Implementing this aspect of the strategy began about three years ago when consultants were brought in to teach selling skills to the employees. Underlying the strong sales orientation that the consultants taught was the idea that *sales brings the customers into the store but service keeps them.* According to Gunn, in 1985 net new personal checking accounts were a negative 9,700. In 1986 that figure improved to a negative 5,600 net new accounts. However, since the inception of the sales orientation, that figure has turned positive. In 1987 net new accounts amounted to 9,900; in 1988, 14,800; in 1989, 32,000. In 1990 net new accounts were even higher.

A unique aspect of the sales training was the development of Seafirst College, patterned after McDonald's Hamburger U. Seafirst College was established with the help of the faculty of the Graduate School of Business at the University of Washington. Instructors at the college are comprised of both university faculty and Seafirst's own training and development staff. As of Fall

1989, more than 500 of Seafirst's personal bankers have completed the course work at Seafirst College.

At the heart of this training effort is, "How to Manage a Franchise," designed to empower the branch manager to run a branch that is responsive to local market conditions. This is a crucial aspect of Seafirst's strategy. *While product is standardized across the system, service is not.* Service is tailored to the specific nuances of the market in which the branch is operating. The rationale for this is simple. According to Helms, "Many consumers in Washington display animosity toward banks that are headquartered in out-of-state cities. In such banks, consumer and business loans typically are approved at the regional or headquarters level, rather than within the branch." The franchise concept gave Seafirst a significant competitive edge in this regard. It enabled Seafirst to compete not as a monolithic corporate giant but as a family of 183 community banks or branches.

For example, at one Seafirst branch location which serves a market dominated by commercial fishermen, branch employees accept a commercial fisherman's license as identification, instead of a driver's license. The reason for this is clear. Seafirst knows that many commercial fishermen do not drive. "We're probably the only bank that does that. It's one of the reasons that makes us different," suggests one teller.

Personal Bankers are rigorously screened through a video taping process. "We video tape every single personal banker and hire only on the basis of the video tape and not on the basis of background. We just want to see friendly people," Helms said.

Supporting this sales orientation is a strong portfolio of market driven products. Product development is the responsibility of the corporate side of the bank and not the branch. An example is the Peak Certificate of Deposit which offers customers a high, fixed rate of interest for a short period, followed by a variable rate structure. The product was on the market within one week of its conceptualization instead of the more typical three-month gestation period. The product has produced more than 75,000 accounts totaling $900 million in deposits. Each product concept is carefully scrutinized for its ability to provide a needed service to the customer. According to Helms, "Everything we sell will have service standards. If we can't meet those standards, we won't sell the product!"

Balancing this aggressive sales orientation is a deep and genuine desire to help customers, which is compatible with the sales ethic. "We're not here just to sell them products but to help them. The idea is to know your 'clients' well enough to identify them as prospects for future promotions," related one branch manager. "We are relationship officers—that is what really distinguishes us. Most other banks don't have this follow through," said another.

Helms proudly pointed out the following:

> By the end of 1988, Seafirst was able to report earnings of $159.2 million, which includes a one-time extraordinary gain of $50.3 million. The bank's goal had been to achieve $100 million in earnings by the end of the decade, so the fact that Seafirst reached its goal two years ahead of schedule suggests that the changes in cost control and sales orientation are working.

Incentives provide the selling motivation for Seafirst employees. The bank devised a variable incentive plan that changes as products, employee expertise, and profit levels change.

Phase Three: "We Make Banking Easier for You"

Making banking easier for the customer is the goal of Seafirst's customer service initiative. While quick to point out that they are not there yet, Helms added with certain satisfaction and conviction, "We're killing the competition, absolutely killing them!"

The cost cutting and sales efforts, however, had given Seafirst a temporary competitive advantage. To solidify that advantage, Seafirst knew from its research that it would have to become the number one customer service bank in the markets in which it operated. Whichever bank could be the first in the market with an innovative service program offering the right combination of service elements would be the winner.

Excel Service

Excel Service was the vehicle to make Seafirst number one. Excel Service is driven by two objectives: a focus on service and the element of speed. Excel Service is a combination of customer service programs involving 24-hour person-to-person checking, extended branch hours, a five-minute service guarantee, and a commitment to excellence in courtesy.

The 24-hour telephone service provides the customer access to more than 100 types of transactions seven days a week. Each branch is equipped with courtesy phones for its walk-in customers. The telephone service facility now handles over 11,000 calls each day!

Extended branch hours were the product of research indicating a need to bank after work and on Saturdays. All Seafirst branches are open from 9 AM to 6 PM Monday through Friday and from 9 AM to 1 PM on Saturday. In keeping with the philosophy of managing independent franchises, branch managers are free to establish longer hours if they are needed. Devotion to the objective of exceptional service was so strong that Seafirst management even looked at opening on Sunday, however, research indicated that customer interest was not sufficient to do so.

The 5-minute or $5 feature offers customers $5 if they have to wait in line more than 5 minutes. This has cost Seafirst, to date, $61,000, a much lower figure than expected. To make this work Seafirst hired more tellers and introduced the idea of express lines. In addition, all branch personnel were trained to step in and staff the teller positions as needed to meet customer demands. Even branch managers were supplied with their own cash cans.

The emphasis on courtesy was also generated from research findings. Seafirst's surveys showed that customers valued aspects of courtesy such as establishing eye contact, smiling, and calling the client by name. Figure 8-1 is a sample of the "Excellence in Courtesy" poster used to train employees.

The Philosophy that Drives Excel Service

While Excel Service has been successful for Seafirst, it is simply the manifestation of an almost fanatical and slavish devotion to a clear vision of banking held by Luke Helms. In talking to Helms about customer service, there is little doubt that he is truly committed to providing the best customer service possible.

Figure 8-1
Excellence in Courtesy Training Piece

EXCELLENCE
IN
COURTESY

SERVICE TEAM

Smile
Eye Contact
Name of Client
Thank the Client
Smile

SALES TEAM

Stand
Eye Contact
Extend Hands
Name of Client
Seat the Client

Figure 8-1
Excellence in Courtesy Training Piece *continued*

- **Greetings that make "SENTS" for Tellers**
- **Award winning "SEENS" for Sellers**

1. Introduction—What's in a Name?

Once there was a Greek general who knew more than 10,000 warriors by name. They say he did it because although it took a lot of effort, he thought he would be paid back immeasurably by his men's loyalty. And he was right! His success in battle and the loyalty of his men became legendary. At Seafirst, nobody will expect one person to know 10,000 clients by name, but we want to achieve that same feeling of loyalty from them.

Everyone likes to hear their own name. It makes us feel important, recognized, and acknowledged. That's why using clients' names is such a key part of our commitment to excellence in courtesy.

Every year Seafirst conducts a survey to assess customer satisfaction. The 1988 Customer Satisfaction Survey has told us two things:

1. Our clients like to be addressed by name, and
2. We need to do a better job doing that.

That is the reason for providing this short training piece. It is designed to help us with strategies and raps to enhance the feeling that our clients are not just another transaction, but are special. The focus here will be on using the client's name. Subsequent training will give additional practical help on memory techniques.

2. Expectations for Tellers and Sellers

It is imperative that we create a comfortable, caring environment in our branches for our clients. Therefore, it is necessary that we show our clients the courtesy of recognizing them when they enter the branch and calling them by name.

Expectations of the Tellers are to use **Greetings that make "SENTS."**

Smile
Eye Contact
Name
Thank You
Smile

SMILE When we look up and are ready to address a client, our first reaction should **always** be to smile.

EYE CONTACT The way to snow sincerity and demonstrate that we are giving the client our undivided attention is to **always** gain eye contact.

NAME Here is our opportunity to give the client our personal touch. If we are already aware of the client's name, we use it immediately in the greeting and **again** in the closing of the transaction. If we do not know the client, we look for the name in the course of the transaction and use it before the client leaves the work area.

Figure 8-1
Excellence in Courtesy Training Piece *continued*

THANK YOU There is never a case when we should not thank the client. Thanking the client with conviction is as important as balancing at the end of the day or any other part of everyday duties. Be sincere. Where would we be without our clients?

SMILE Saying "Thank you" goes naturally with a pleasant smile. This brings us full circle—we begin and end each client contact with a smile.

EXAMPLE: A client walks up to our window. We **SMILE**, make **EYE CONTACT**, and might say, "Good morning, how may I help you?" We look at the transaction to find the **NAME**, and say, "How are your today, Mr. Bradshaw?" After completing the transaction, we **THANK** the client, using their name. "Mr. Bradshaw, thank you for banking at Seafirst." And we **SMILE** as they leave.

While the Sellers must also provide the same courtesy exhibited by Greetings that make "SENTS", they must extend an additional effort to furnish excellent service. Expectations of the Sellers are to create **Award winning "SEENS."**

Stand and Smile
Eye Contact
Extend Hand
Name
Seat Client

STAND & SMILE When a client steps up to the desk, we **always** stand and greet with a smile. If we greet a client while we are seated, we send a message that we are too busy or not ready to give them undivided attention.

EYE CONTACT We are reenforcing the idea of **eye contact**. We want to show a client that we are sincere and appreciate their business. Eye contact is one of the best ways to tell our clients that we are giving them our attention. We are **never** to ignore a client. If we see a client in our area, that person is our **first priority**. We want to put aside what we are doing, and meet the needs of the client. If we are already with a client, we are still capable of making eye contact with the second client, and some indication that we know they are there. In that way, the second client does not feel ignored.

EXTEND HAND Making our clients feel comfortable is one of our greatest responsibilities. By using a firm hand shake we show that we care.

NAME While shaking hands, we make an introduction. "Good morning, I'm Sally Seller. I'm a Seafirst _____. I like to get to know all of my clients personally. May I ask your name?" "I'm happy to meet you, Mr. _____." We only use their first name if the client requests it.

SEAT CLIENT When we have completed all of the previous steps, we invite the client to be seated. We don't assume that they will automatically sit down. We want to make them feel as comfortable in our branch as they would feel in our home.

Figure 8-1
Excellence in Courtesy Training Piece *continued*

It is important to understand that a "Thank you" and a smile are just as important for the Sellers as for Tellers. After the transaction has been finalized, we want to show appreciation by thanking the client. A smile is automatic when a "Thank you" is sincere.

We all remember things that are important to us. Why wouldn't we make an effort to remember our clients, upon whom we all depend for our livelihoods?

There are two major things we can do to remember to use:
Greetings that make "SENTS" and Awarding winning "SEENS".
1. **Memorize** the acronyms, "SENTS" and "SEENS" and what they stand for.
2. **Practice**, starting immediately, with clients that come into the branch. It might also be good to practice with co-workers. For example, do you know, by name, everyone that you come into contact with at the branch? If not, ask their names and practice in your normal conversation. Instead of asking, "Do you know the current estimated yield on the Peak?", try, "Becky, do you know...?" Everyone likes to hear their own name, and practice will help us establish the habit.

By far, the most important thing we can do to remember a client's name is to **repeat** it. It would be good to use it **naturally** a couple of times in a conversation. Some typical examples might be:
1. "Good afternoon, Mrs. Peterson."
2. "Mrs. Peterson, your account balance is..."
3. "Mrs. Peterson, I notice you have a very substantial balance in your savings account. Were you aware that we have other investments that can give you a greater return?"
4. "Mrs. Peterson, thank you for coming in. Is there anything else we can do for you?"

Often it can be helpful to say the client's name first, as in the final example. This ensures that we will clearly say the client's name, and not mumble or swallow it, as we might do if it were the last part of a sentence. Some people very effectively use the following technique: say the client's name, **pause** for just a brief instant, and finish the sentence. For example, "Miss Fernandez-(slight pause)-have a great day!"

3. **Sample Situations in Using the Client's Name**

The following example illustrates how we can use the client's name in various situations.
"What if...?"
- the client is a lot younger than me? I feel silly saying "Mr. Jones, thank you," to someone who's 20 when I'm 45.

The Seafirst commitment to excellence in courtesy means that every client, regardless of age, be treated with the same formal respect unless the client has requested that we address them by their first name.

In the structure of his thinking is the basic proposition that, *"The bank team, from teller to executive, needs to focus on customer service first and banking second."* This priority position of customer service is manifested in the Seafirst Mission Statement. Figure 8-2 is a sample of this statement.

While innovative market driven products are important to Seafirst and its overall strategy, Helms is quick to point out that overreliance on a product driven banking strategy is foolish. "We don't sell products. You don't see us advertising products. There is no lock on products in this business. *The key is service and there is a lock on service."*

Helms goes on to explain that service standards are being imposed on banking whether individual bank managements care to admit it or not:

> If a bank president thinks that he or she has any control over the level of service that their customers demand, they are going to lose. In the Northwest we are blessed with some outstanding service companies. A customer that is going to bank at Seafirst may have already done business with Nordstroms, or shopped at QFC (Quality Food Centers) or Larry's, or may have picked up someone who just flew in on Alaska Airlines. Holy cow! All of a sudden you go to a bank where some stiff says "can I help you?" or you have to wait in a line that's 20 miles long. The customer is going to say why can't I get the same level of quality service in my bank that I get elsewhere?
>
> Go to McDonald's. How can McDonald's be so damn good? They're selling a stupid hamburger. What restaurant in the U.S. doesn't or can't sell hamburgers? How can they feed 10% of the American population every day? It's amazing. If you walk into a McDonald's, and we all do it when we're out visiting the branches, we even share parking lots with them in some of our locations, the speed and the level of service that you get is something else. *If our customer's expectations are being raised by companies that really know what they are doing, we're going to lose if we don't hit just the bare minimums.*

Figure 8-2
Seafirst Mission Statement

SEAFIRST MISSION STATEMENT

Seafirst's Management Committee recently spent three days looking at where we have been over the past year and where we hope to go in the next 12 months.

Out of those meetings came a reiteration that our mission statement is as true and important as it has ever been. For your benefit, we've reprinted it below.

Seafirst's Mission is to be the premier Northwest bank, providing the highest quality customer service, achieving superior profitability and dominant market share in the Pacific Northwest personal, business, and real estate markets.

The achievement of quality customer service will be measured by periodic customer surveys. Profitability will be measured in comparison to our peer banks. Market share will also be measured by periodic surveys. The results of these measurements will be reported on a regular basis to the board of directors and to staff.

Seafirst's staff is the single most important resource employed in accomplishing the mission. Since all of us are responsible for our success, Seafirst will continue to provide an environment that encourages each of us to be successful and enables each of us to achieve our full potential.

Helms believes that location and image are the responsibility of the corporate headquarters staff, while sales and service are the branches' business. One of the biggest problems he faces is over management of the branch operations from headquarters. Using an auto corporation model this time Helms explained:

> Conceptually, I work for Ford Motor in Detroit. I don't own the dealerships. But I'll design the cars, I'll do the image advertising, and I'll pick the franchises. All you have to do is sell so much in a professional manner for a certain price. One of the hardest things is getting people who work on this floor to realize that those branches do not report to anyone on this floor. *Those are independent entrepreneurs. Don't bother them. Leave them alone and you'll get the best customer service in the world.* If someone has a complaint, handle it on your own just like someone would do if they owned a business. We're betting on the future. We have the locations and the cost structure and now we have the service ethic. No one can beat us.

Helms appears to know what he is talking about; Seafirst is acquiring about 10,000 to 12,000 new customers a month.

This "hands-off support" at the corporate level has not always worked smoothly. Marie Gunn related what happens when there is a breakdown between front line operations and the support side of the organization. This example also points out how an effective recovery operates.

> The back room processing issue is a big one. Our sales force got really powerful and we didn't have the back room to support it. The problem was that none of us at the corporate level knew that the sales force was that powerful. We had a home equity campaign with a number of really aggressive goals and the back room said we could support those goals. The branches blew the doors off of every goal and the back room got buried. The clients were furious because the loans weren't closing. It was a disaster. Branches were mad at us and mad at everybody. But as a result of that, we hired people to set up a separate home equity center called "Quick Silver" which has a guaranteed turnaround time. No one ever dreamed that would have happened.

We also had a similar situation which turned into a disaster. We offer a CD at a great rate on Saturday only. We call them "Saturday Specials." Branches called their portfolio clients. This one Saturday we offered one that wasn't really that great a rate so we added four free tickets on a cruise that just goes up to Victoria. It's a day cruise. The tickets were provided by a new cruise company that wanted the business. The staff predicted that we would sell 5,000 to 6,000 CDs but we sold 11,000! The cruise company couldn't book all those customers. We let them down and we let them down badly. I took a lot of those complaints. I sent each a box of chocolates and a personal note. The customers loved it! The problem is that the systems haven't been there to support the branches. The branches feel it because they have to talk to the customers. They didn't let the customer down. We did. We're in the process of fixing the system and giving them the support they need.

Customer Retention

But customer acquisition alone is not sufficient. Customer retention is a crucial aspect to how Seafirst conducts business. Helms made this point very clear:

I tell Earl (Earl Shulman is Vice Chairman in charge of the branches) all the time: you get no credit when the branches come in and say we opened 12,000 checking accounts last month. You tell me how many closed. That's where service comes in. We're still closing way too many accounts, way too many. Look at it this way. Anytime Earl gets about a three percent improvement in customer retention at this bank it's equal to a fully mature branch that has been here for five, six, or seven years. How hard is that? It's really hard but the numbers are there. If we can bring in 12,000 customers a month and he can cut the losses to 6,000 a month, then every month we are adding about 6,000 customers and that's where it's at.

Gunn addressed the problems of managing customer retention:

> It's difficult for the branch managers to manage the retention side of the equation. Branches are still uncomfortable with our retention goals. They know when they've made a sale, but they don't know when they've saved an account because they handled a complaint well. So it's harder to get that across. We talk to them a lot about complaint handling and how important it is. In my office we end up with a lot of corporate level complaints which is fine because they shouldn't be bothered with issues at that level.

Helms also pointed out:

> About 75% of our customers come to Seafirst because they are unhappy with the way they have been treated somewhere else. Our customers are running out the door going to Security Pacific and their customers are running headlong into ours who are trying to get into their bank. They're running to find that good service.

How does Helms envision his role in the culture change? He explained that it is essentially the CEO's responsibility to decide upon the course of action and then give people the resources to accomplish the change. "How can you make a mistake in becoming a customer service bank? You might make a mistake in implementation but you can't make a mistake in giving customers good service." He sees his job as essentially an asset allocation job.

Shulman gave the following point of view:

> You essentially have to do it, eat it, breathe it, live it every day. The troops need to see you doing it. It's a leadership issue. You have to tell them a zillion times what we are trying to do and why. There isn't a group in the bank that I talk to that

does not hear about cost, sales, and service. The other thing is that both of us, and all the people running this bank, have to be in touch with the customer. We all take complaints and customer calls. It's the one way that you find out the perspective of what is really happening.

Sales and Service at the Store Level

How does the philosophy of Luke Helms and the strategic planning of Seafirst translate into customer service at the branch level? To answer that question all you have to do is talk to the branch managers and the tellers. And, when you do, you will find that several key factors make Excel Service operational. Some of those factors include the Service Heroes Program, empowering employees to make account adjustments and tracking service quality.

Service Heroes

Service Heroes is a program for recognizing excellence in service on the part of individual employees throughout the bank. People can nominate any individual on the service staff for the award. Each month each team leader will choose 10 employees who will receive a $50 award, a certificate, and a commendation in their personnel file. Figure 8-3 is a sample of the Service Heroes program description.

The following are two examples of Service Heroes at Seafirst. Rey is a teller who has been recognized for his excellent service. He is also a Service Hero. Rey was recognized for his treatment of a customer who had a flat tire. While Seafirst is bullish on customer service, Rey demonstrated the type of behavior that is nowhere in the job description of a teller.

Rey was at his teller position when he saw a customer who had a flat tire. Rey changed the tire for the customer. The next week, Rey helped a lady who had a problem with her carburetor. Rey is a little embarrassed when he tells the story of how he was able to help the customer who had locked his keys in the car. The customer had been trying to get into the car for about half an hour when Rey saw him. Rey had the door open in about five minutes.

Figure 8-3
Service Heroes

BRANCH CUSTOMER SERVICE STAFF RECOGNITION PROGRAM DESCRIPTION

Program Objective
To recognize and reward those front-line customer service staff for meritorious service to our customers and outstanding professional performance.

Eligibility
All tellers, CSR positions, and Customer Service Managers.

"How It Works"
When a branch manager (managers might also ask their customer service managers to be watchful as well) sees or hears of an outstanding customer experience from one of these eligible staff:

- Complete a *Service Hero Coupon* and present the top ply directly to the staff member in as timely manner as possible to the excellent customer event.
- Let the staff member know that in addition to the branch manager's recognition of the staff member's fine job in servicing that customer, the branch manager will submit the staff member's name and a description of the customer event to that branch's team leader for nomination for reward and corporate-wide publication.
- Next complete the second ply of the *Service Hero Coupon* with a brief description of the customer event and send it to the branch's team leader.
- At the end of each month, each team leader will select the 10 most outstanding customer service experiences from those branch nominees. The staff member selected by the team leader will receive a letter of thanks from Consumer Banking Group Manager Earl Shulman and a check for $50. In addition, the staff member's name will appear in *Seafirst News* as one of that month's "Service Heroes."

Examples of a Service Hero
These are only examples; the fact is that branch managers really recognize outstanding customer service when it's seen. But the following may help:

- Someone who recognizes a potential error in a customer's account and corrects it before it occurs.
- Someone who turns an irate customer who's ready to walk out the door and take all their money with them into a satisfied customer who wants to not only keep their existing accounts but wants to transfer additional funds from another bank.
- Someone who delivers something to a customer when they are unable to make it into the bank (goes out of their way on their own time).
- When a customer takes the time to inform you that one of your employees has done something special for them.
- When a customer has what they feel to be a complex, confusing transaction and your employee is able to not only accommodate the customer but also is able to show them a much easier method for future transactions.

Figure 8-3
Service Heroes continued

Congratulations

SERVICE HERO

YOU'VE JUST "*Added a Plus*" AND CREATED AN EXTRAORDINARY CUSTOMER EXPERIENCE.

MANAGER'S SIGNATURE   BRANCH/DEPT.   DATE

FORM 2999 10/89

The customer looked at Rey in disbelief at his skill at opening locked car doors. Rey felt obligated to assure the customer that he did not do this kind of work professionally.

Holly is another example of customer service at work at Seafirst. Needless to say she is also a Service Hero. Holly's branch manager told about the time she was working on a note for a young couple:

> We had some difficulty in getting the loan documents together. I finally got them together and his wife happened to have a baby that same day. They couldn't come in to sign the papers. So I had them redocumented for another time when I was going to be out of the branch. I put all of the documents in a big envelope and put them in our kiosk, which is our greeter area. When the husband came into the bank to pick them up, no one could find them. Later that day Holly found the papers and felt sorry that this young man had made a special trip into the bank. He had to leave his wife only to find that no one knew where the papers were. Holly took the paperwork out of the envelope, looked at the address and saw that it wasn't too far from where she lived. So she took the papers with her. She knocked on his door and he opened it, holding his brand new little baby. Here was Holly to personally deliver the papers. He was really, really pleased. Of course I was thankful because we would have had to redocument the papers again.

Why does Seafirst get such dedication from its employees? One teller explained it the following way:

> It's important when your supervisor and your manager notice you making the effort. It's so much easier to be nice to another person when your supervisor gives you the strokes so that you have them to give to the customer. Obviously you have to come in with a good attitude. When you have people who are right behind you or right next to you on the teller line who acknowledge good customer service, it feeds on itself. If you have that from the top down in your branch, then you'll give it to your customers.

One branch manager went so far as to say, "we try to catch people giving outstanding service. When I find someone who is doing that, I make a special effort to recognize it."

All of this produces a strong corporate commitment to customer service on the part of management and employees. What Helms called a "service ethic" is a highly palpable feeling when talking to people in the branches. There is a strong sense of teamwork that binds both manager and employee. As one teller indicated, "the managers are on the front line with everybody else. The clients love it, they just love it."

Reinforcing this service ethic is the recognition that employees at Seafirst not only serve "external customers" but also "internal customers." Employees who have received excellent service from other Seafirst individuals acknowledge this service by sending them a "Thank you for making it easier" memo. Figure 8-4 is a sample of this memo. It communicates to other Seafirst employees the appreciation felt by others who are impacted by their work. In so doing, it provides employees with a "bigger picture" of their contribution while fostering a stronger sense of teamwork.

Empowering Employees to Give Service

One other aspect of the service delivery system merits attention. This has to do with the corporate emphasis on customer retention and what Gunn referred to as "recovery". Each teller at Seafirst is empowered to make account adjustments up to $50. They are permitted to reverse fees, refund fees or checks, adjust NSF charges, and make interest adjustments—no questions are asked. Helms argues that if the issue ever reaches him he will make the change himself, so why not make it at the point of service interface and do it quickly? According to the tellers and the branch managers, the reaction of the customers is one of amazement. The tellers said that their customers are flabbergasted that they are able to take care of their problems so quickly and so surprised that they don't have to go through an endless process of obtaining approval from superiors. Customer service is such

Figure 8-4
"Thank You For Making It Easier" Memo

Thank You For Making It Easier.

To ______________________ Branch / Dept. ______________

How You Made It Easier ______________________________

____

____

______________ ______________ ______________
From Branch / Dept Date

SEAFIRST BANK
Member FDIC
We Make It Easy For You

Original - Send to Recipient

Copy - Send to Quality of Service, FAB - 28

FORM 4015 09/90

an important factor in the Seafirst business philosophy that it would take a really significant sum of money before Seafirst would be willing to jeopardize a customer relationship.

Tracking Service Quality

One of the keys to insuring that the service quality standards are being met is the comprehensive tracking system that Seafirst employs. Customers are surveyed when they open accounts and when they apply for a Seafirst Bank card. This feedback lets branch managers know how well branch employees are meeting basic service standards. Figure 8-5 is a sample of the survey forms used.

At the heart of the monitoring system is the annual survey conducted by Marie Gunn. A survey of 67,000 clients is conducted every year to gauge the level of service Seafirst is providing its customers. Figure 8-6 is an example of how clients rated Seafirst. This information is analyzed on a branch by branch basis in Figure 8-7. (These figures are excerpts from Seafirst's employee newsletter, *Seafirst News*.)

It is interesting to note the perceptions of changes in the level of service that Seafirst is providing. Fifty-seven percent of those interviewed felt that the level of service had improved from last year. Forty percent felt that it had stayed about the same while only 3% felt that it had decreased! These are impressive numbers.

In addition, Seafirst has implemented a shoppers program to be conducted by an outside company. Each branch will be shopped four times a year in person and four times by phone. "The objective of the program," according to Gunn, "is to give branch managers a tool to measure and monitor the service level provided in their franchises."

How does the shoppers program translate into bottom line evidence that customer service pays? Helms proudly pointed out:

> Seafirst feels that it is on the right track with its cost-control, sales, and service strategies. The bank's 1989 earnings continue to set records, market share is increasing, employee morale is high, and consumer enthusiasm is evident. Above all, con-

Figure 8-5
Seafirst Customer Service Survey Forms

1. Thinking about your banking relationship with Seafirst, how important are each of the following factors in maintaining that relationship? (Circle one number for each factor.)

	Not at all Important			Very Important	
Prices/rates	1	2	3	4	5
Customer service	1	2	3	4	5
Convenience (location or hours)	1	2	3	4	5
Wide variety of products or services offered	1	2	3	4	5

2. Which Seafirst branch do you visit most often? (If unsure of name, give city and cross streets of the branch location.)

   _____

3. Is the Seafirst branch you visit most often closer to
   ❒ Home   ❒ Work   ❒ School?

4. Overall, how would you rate the service you receive at the **Seafirst** branch you visit most often?

	Poor			Excellent	
Overall satisfaction with service	1	2	3	4	5

5. To what extent does the service you receive at this branch match your expectations?
   ❒ Consistently exceeds expectations
   ❒ Meets expectations
   ❒ Consistently does not meet expectations

6. Now, please rate the staff at the Seafirst branch you go to most often. Indicate how the staff performs in the following areas: (Circle the appropriate rating.)

	Poor				Excellent
Greeting and acknowledging you promptly	1	2	3	4	5
Addressing you by name	1	2	3	4	5
Providing friendly, caring service	1	2	3	4	5
Serving you quickly and efficiently	1	2	3	4	5
Handling your transactions accurately	1	2	3	4	5
Providing clear explanations of services	1	2	3	4	5
Being flexible	1	2	3	4	5
Solving problems/troubleshooting	1	2	3	4	5
Thanking you for your business	1	2	3	4	5

Figure 8-5
Seafirst Customer Service Survey Forms *continued*

7. If you could change or improve anything at this Seafirst branch, what would it be?

   _____

   _____

   _____

8. Would you say that quality of service provided by Seafirst overall has improved, stayed the same, or decreased in the past year?
   ❒ Improved   ❒ Stayed the same   ❒ Decreased

9. Do you consider Seafirst to be your primary financial institution (that is, where you conduct the majority of your banking)?
   ❒ Yes ❒ No

10. How long have you been a customer of Seafirst?
   ❒ Less than six months   ❒ Three to five years
   ❒ Six months to one year ❒ Five to ten years
   ❒ One to three years   ❒ Ten years or more

11. What is your age?
   ❒ Under 18 ❒ 25-34 ❒ 45-54 ❒ 65-74
   ❒ 18-24   ❒ 35-44 ❒ 55-64 ❒ 75 or older

12. Which of the following categories best describes your yearly household income?
   ❒ Under $20,000   ❒ $50,000-$74,999
   ❒ $20,000-$34,999   ❒ $75,000-$99,999
   ❒ $35,000-$49,999   ❒ $100,000 or more

Thank You For Your Help!

Figure 8-5
Seafirst Customer Service Survey Forms *continued*

10/25/90

John Doe
Jane Doe
Sample Street
Anytown, USA 12345

Dear Seafirst Client,

On behalf of Seafirst Bank, I'd like to personally thank you for opening your new FirstChoice Interest Checking account at the Vashon Island Branch. We are pleased to have the opportunity to serve you.

By choosing Seafirst, you've given us a chance to show you what we mean by Excel Service. Our goal is to meet your highest expectations, providing you with a more convenient, more pleasant way to do your banking.

We are always trying to improve the service we provide our customers. And for that reason, I've enclosed a brief questionnaire. If you would complete and return it to us in the postage-paid envelope, it would help us do an even better job for you.

Again, thank you for choosing Seafirst. If there's anything we can do for you, please don't hesitate to call on us. You may reach Seafirst Customer Service at 1-800-442-6680 (in Seattle 461-0800) anytime of the day or night. Or, visit any branch from 9:00 AM to 6:00 PM Monday through Friday and Saturdays from 9:00 AM to 1:00 PM.

Sincerely,

Quality of Service Manager

Figure 8-5
Seafirst Customer Service Survey Forms *continued*

WE WANT TO HEAR FROM YOU

Overall, how would you rate the service you have received so far at Seafirst?

POOR				EXCELLENT
1	2	3	4	5

To what extent did our service meet your expectations?
❐ EXCEEDED   ❐ MET   ❐ DID NOT MEET
How might we have served you better?

_____

	YES	NO
Did your checks arrive within 10 days of opening your account?	❐	❐
Were your checks printed as ordered?	❐	❐
Was the check style the one you selected?	❐	❐
Was your first statement completely accurate?	❐	❐
Did you find your statement easy to read?	❐	❐
Did you find your cash machine card and personal identification number (PIN) arrive within 7 days?	❐	❐

When opening your checking account, how well were the account and its features explained to you?

NOT AT ALL WELL			VERY WELL	
1	2	3	4	5

	YES	NO
When you opened your new account, were additional Seafirst services explained to you?	❐	❐

If not, your specific suggestions would be appreciated:

_____

If you would like to have a Personal Banker call, please check one or both of the boxes below and provide your name, address, and daytime phone number:
❐   I want to discuss changes or corrections to my account.
❐   I want more information on Seafirst services.

Name	Daytime Phone	
Address		
City	State	Zip

Figure 8-5
Seafirst Customer Service Survey Forms *continued*

Dear Seafirst Client:

On behalf of Seafirst Bank, thank you for selecting us for your credit card relationship. Now that you have received your Visa or MasterCard, we would like to find out how you think we are doing.

At Seafirst, customer feedback is very important to us. Our goal is to exceed your highest expectations and that is why I've enclosed a brief questionnaire. It only takes a few minutes to complete and your participation would be appreciated. When you're finished, just return the questionnaire in the postage-paid envelope.

If there's anything we can do for you, please call our customer service representatives at 1-800-552-7302.

Again, thank you for choosing Seafirst. We are pleased to have the opportunity to serve you.

Sincerely,

Quality of Service Manager

Figure 8-5
Seafirst Customer Service Survey Forms *continued*

WE WOULD LIKE TO HEAR FROM YOU

1. Overall, how would you rate the service you have received so far from Seafirst Bankcard Services? (Circle one number.)

    POOR   EXCELLENT
    1   2   3   4   5

2. When you considered applying for a credit card, why did you select Seafirst? (Please explain.) _____

    _____

3. To what extent do you agree or disagree with the following statements? (Circle one number for each.)

    STRONGLY   STRONGLY
    DISAGREE   AGREE

    The application was very easy to complete. 1   2   3   4   5
    I received approval for my credit card in a
    timely manner.   1   2   3   4   5
    My credit line is sufficient for my needs.   1   2   3   4   5
    I received my credit card in a timely
    manner.   1   2   3   4   5

4. Did you receive your personal identification number (PIN) within four business days of receiving your card? (Circle yes or no.)

    YES   NO

5. If you have received your first credit card statement, was it completely accurate? (Circle yes or no.)   YES   NO

6. How would you rate your statement in terms of being easy to read and understand? (Circle one number.)

    VERY   VERY
    DIFFICULT   EASY
    1   2   3   4   5

Figure 8-5
Seafirst Customer Service Survey Forms *continued*

7. If you are not completely satisfied with your statement, do you have any suggestions for how it could be made easier to read and understand? (Please explain.)

_____

_____

_____

_____

8. Do you have any suggestions for how we could improve your Seafirst credit card? For example, are there any other features you would like us to offer?

_____

_____

_____

_____

(Optional) Name:_____

Account Number:_____

The following code only tells us your account type. It does not identify you personally.

Figure 8-6
Seafirst Annual Survey Results

'OUTSTANDING'

ACCORDING TO OUR CUSTOMERS, 1989 WAS A GREAT YEAR FOR SERVICE

E very year Seafirst asks our clients to tell us how we did. And for 1989, our customers told us we did a great job providing them high quality service.

A revamped and revised one-page survey mailed to 67,000 clients used a new scale of one (poor) to five (excellent) and replaced the '88 four-page survey which used a rating scale of zero to eight to measure customer satisfaction.

"The bank's overall satisfaction score is 4.45," says Marie Gunn, Quality of Service manager. "Nine out of 10 clients gave us a rating of four or five and over half our clients feel our service has improved over last year.

"Our clients gave high ratings for our accuracy, and

feel our service has improved," says Earl Shulman, Consumer Banking Group manager. "Although Excel Service played a big role for our clients, the outstanding ratings certainly reflect

IMPORTANT RELATIONSHIP FACTORS	
Customer Service	4.65
Convenience (location or hours)	4.55
Prices/rates	4.36
Wide variety of products or services	3.75

we scored well in acknowledging clients promptly, thanking them for their business, and the quickness and efficiency of service we provided," she says.

"It is impressive that more than half of the respondents

Our clients gave high ratings for our accuracy, and we scored well in acknowledging clients promptly,...and the quickness and efficiency of service we provided.

everybody's hard work at providing good service."

Additional surveys were distributed in branches, asking them to grade us for 1989. "Surveys were mailed to a sampling of our depositors," explains Gunn. "We

received 16,109 surveys back and it was from these that the results of the survey were compiled. Unfortunately, because of the timing, we were unable to include the American Savings branches."

Other results show that nine out of 10 clients surveyed consider Seafirst to be their primary bank with 24 percent joining us within the past three years. Fifty-seven percent indicated they've been with the bank 10 years or more.

Eastern Region scores exceeded those for Western Region on every factor measured, "probably because so many Eastern Region branches are located in smaller, closer-knit communities," says Gunn.

Western Region clients were more motivated by convenience than their East- *(Continued on page 2)*

Figure 8-6
Seafirst Annual Survey Results *continued*

TOP SERVICE

(Continued from page 1)

ern Region counterparts, but Eastern Region clients attached a greater importance to prices and rates and the wide variety of products or services available.

CHANGE IN SERVICE FROM LAST YEAR	
Improved	57%
Stayed the same	40%
Decreased	5%

Also, within the Eastern Region, ratings given by Central Team clients exceeded those by Eastern Team clients on all factors. "What the survey told us is that to our clients the most important factor is good customer service," says Gunn. "And one of the areas that needs improvement is addressing our clients by name."

As a result, Quality of

Service is formulating a plan to address this issue. "All the branches will be working on action plans which will help them address areas of concern," explains Shulman.

"Surveys measure the percent of satisfaction and dissatisfaction with an organization's products and services," says Shulman. "I'm very pleased with this year's survey results. The personal efforts of all of our branch staff contributed significantly to these gratifying results."

OVERALL SERVICE RATING	
Overall satisfation with branch visited most often	4.45
Branch Service Consistently exceeds expectations	32%
Meets Expectation	66%
Consistently does not meet expectations	2%

To give you a better idea how our clients rated us, here are the bankwide ratings on some key service qualities and issues. The ratings are graded on a scale of one (poor) to five (excellent).

STAFF SERVICE RATINGS	
Handling your transaction accurately	4.46
Thanking you for your business	4.40
Greeting and acknowledging you promptly	4.40
Serving you quickly and efficiently	4.38
Providing friendly, caring service	4.35
Providing clear explanations of services	4.29
Solving problems/ troubleshooting	4.24
Being flexible	4.17
Addressing by name	3.76

Figure 8-7
Seafirst Survey Branch Results

TOP BRANCHES
CLIENTS RATE OUR SERVICE

According to the results from the annual Seafirst customer survey, the South Bend Branch is tops in keeping their clients happy.

Laurie Hobi, branch manager and a lifetime resident of South Bend, attributes their top rating to "looking at each and every client as if they were the most important client of the bank.

"There are a lot of things that we do that our clients really appreciate and like," she says. "For example, winning their trust, being sensitive to their needs and really taking the time to listen, calling them by name, going out of our way to meet their expectations, and just being ourselves."

Barbara Pfaff, Oakesdale Branch manager, says that knowing their clients very well and giving the very best service possible are two of the qualities that helped put them in second place. "We really listen to our clients' concerns and take immediate action," she explains. "And if we don't have the answer, we make sure we get back to them as soon as possible. But, the most important thing we do is let our clients know that we really appreciate their business."

Also in the top three is the Sedro Woolley branch where Sharon L. Campbell, branch manager, knows what they have to do to be the best in town.

"With six other financial institutions in a town of about 6,300, we know that if we want to maintain the lead in the market we need to be better than the competition," says Campbell. "And the way we do that is that we care about our clients and they always come first.

"Also, it's rare for a client to complete a transaction without hearing about our current promotion, or particular product or service that would benefit them."

Campbell also attributes the branch's high rating to their "strong sense of pride and ownership in the branch and its success."

From the best-ranked down, here's how customers rated branches in terms of overall satisfaction with service:

South Bend	4.90
Oakesdale	4.79
Sedro Woolley	4.78
Wahkiakum County	4.78
Eighth Street	4.77
Coulee Dam	4.77
Edmonds	4.76
Raymond	4.76
Normandy Park	4.75
Darrington	4.74
Leavenworth	4.74
Kingston	4.72
Sultan	4.71
Poulsbo	4.71
Westport	4.71
Chelan	4.71
Lacrosse	4.70
Carnation	4.69
West Poulsbo	4.69
Colfax	4.69

Odessa	4.69	Spokane and Eastern	4.41
South Mercer Island	4.68	Kent East	4.40
Stanwood	4.67	Opportunity	4.40
Forks	4.66	Richland	4.40
Hadlock	4.66	Burien	4.39
Dishman	4.65	Des Moines	4.39
Cle Elum	4.65	Vashon Island	4.39
Hillyard	4.63	Cheney	4.39
Millwood	4.62	Kennewick	4.39
Sixth & Blanchard	4.61	Toppenish	4.39
Snoqualmie	4.61	Aurora Village	4.38
Highland Hills	4.61	Everett Mall	4.38
Kelso	4.61	Greenwood	4.38
Colville	4.60	Lake Hills	4.38
Sumas	4.59	North Bend	4.38
Bucklin Hill	4.59	Dexter Horton	4.37
Lakewood	4.59	Magnolia	4.37
Twin Lakes	4.59	Metropolitan	4.37
Dayton	4.59	White Center	4.37
Canyon Park	4.58	Eastgate	4.37
Sequim	4.58	Pullman	4.37
Sammamish Highlands	4.58	Hawthorne Hills	4.36
Bremerton	4.58	Industrial	4.36
Wenatchee Valley	4.58	Mercer Island	4.35
Monroe	4.57	Old Seattle	4.34
Newport Hills	4.57	Factoria	4.34
Aberdeen	4.57	Yakima Valley	4.34
Lind	4.57	Ballard	4.33
Crown Hill	4.56	East Bremerton	4.33
Sumner	4.56	Lynnwood	4.32
Connell	4.56	Federal Way	4.32
Walla Walla	4.56	Okanogan Valley	4.32
Mt. Vernon	4.54	Juanita	4.30
Main Office at CSC	4.51	Tacoma	4.30
Wilderness Village	4.51	Republic	4.30
North Spokane	4.51	West Seattle	4.29
North Wenatchee	4.51	Overlake Park	4.29
Union Gap	4.51	Renton	4.29
Fourth at Madison	4.49	Omak	4.29
Georgetown	4.49	Madison-Pike	4.28
Centralia	4.49	Roosevelt Way	4.28
Pasco	4.49	Issaquah	4.28
Westwood Village	4.48	Marysville	4.27
Redmond	4.48	Westlake	4.27
Port Orchard	4.48	Kent	4.27
Silverdale	4.48	Woodinville	4.27
Duvall	4.47	Everett	4.26
Moses Lake	4.47	Lake City	4.26
Sunnyside	4.47	Fairwood	4.25
Port Angeles	4.46	Kirkland	4.24
Wedgwood	4.46	Totem Lake	4.24
Mill Plain	4.46	Broadway	4.23
South Hill	4.46	Sixth and Denny	4.23
Clallam Bay	4.45	Longview	4.23
Port Townsend	4.45	Bellingham	4.22
Fisherman's Terminal	4.45	Southcenter	4.22
West Bremerton	4.45	International	4.20
West Olympia	4.45	Columbia City	4.18
Arlington	4.44	Bellevue	4.17
Kenmore	4.44	185th and Aurora	4.16
Plaza 600	4.44	Auburn	4.16
Shelton	4.44	First Hill	4.15
Vancouver	4.44	Queen Anne	4.15
Chewelah	4.44	Design Center	4.10
Mill Creek	4.43	Bonney Lake	4.09
Snohomish	4.43	University	4.08
Bellevue Place	4.43	Sea-Tac	4.08
Skyline Tower	4.43	Rainier Beach	4.01
Olympia	4.43	South Tacoma	3.97
Forest Park	4.42	Aurora	3.94
South Everett	4.42	Eastlake	3.86
Puyallup	4.42	Beacon Hill	3.84
Northgate	4.41		
Security	4.41		

sumer research shows a dramatic, steady improvement in Seafirst's reputation for caring about its customers, for being helpful, and for showing customers friendly and personal attention. These responses suggest that, in orienting itself as a retailer, Seafirst Bank is achieving a competitive advantage that is sustainable.

Lessons from Seafirst

Seafirst Bank has demonstrated several key points regarding outstanding customer service. The first lesson is the commitment that it requires on the part of top management. In talking with Helms or Shulman there is a strong sense that customer service is not only important but that it is absolutely vital. While top management commitment is trumpeted as a vital ingredient to customer service driven organizations in most books on service, its preeminent role is nonetheless unquestionable.

It is not uncommon, however, to find this commitment lacking. In one banking organization that wanted to move in this direction, the CEO asked for an outline of how we would turn his company into a customer service driven company. After outlining our approach, the CEO said he could not spare his top management people to participate in the training. This dooms any effort from the very start. How important is servicing the customer to this CEO if he or his top people are not willing to participate? How important do you think the rest of the organization will feel customer service is if top management doesn't participate? This is an undeniable truth of customer service driven organizations. **Top management is not involved, they are committed**.

Luke Helms' commitment is unmistakable. Even when he talks about customer service and its role in banking his voice rises several decibels and his speech quickens. He is absolutely convinced of the logic of high quality service.

Another lesson we can learn from Seafirst concerns the idea that *"Before You Can Make a Great Dream Come True You First Have to Have a Great Dream!"* This is what many management gurus call "vision." Helms' vision is crystal clear when he equates banking to retailing and more specifically to McDonald's. His concept of franchise banking, with a strong sales orientation, is vital to the implementation of his strategy. This vision is so clear that every employee that we talked with used the same model for discussing his or her duties in the organization. Seafirst College is an embodiment of Helms' vision of banking. Seafirst College is patterned after Hamburger U, with a heavy emphasis on how to run a franchise. This is also an unmistakable hallmark of his commitment to the concept of franchise banking and the importance of customer service to its success.

It's not uncommon for organizations to have an unclear understanding or picture of what they should look like or be doing in the next five years. It is, however, critical to have this information in an environment that is characterized by instability. Without a clear vision of the organization, there is a strong possibility that the company will flounder, moving from one direction to another without any real purpose.

One of the keys to Seafirst's current success lies in the ability of the tellers and the branch personnel to give the kind of service that distinguishes them from other organizations. The idea of empowering employees to deliver high quality service is just catching on in corporate America. It requires management to trust and respect the ability of their employees. It requires management to understand that they are there to serve the employees in the delivery of high quality customer service. Management may have an input into the creation of service, but it is the front line employee that delivers it.

Finally what can be learned from Seafirst is the idea that "*If You Can't Measure It, You Can't Manage It.*" Seafirst spends significant sums of money on monitoring its performance. Its annual survey queries 67,000 customers. The results of the survey are disseminated to the individual branches for the purpose of providing information on the strengths and weaknesses of their performance. Strengths are rewarded, weaknesses analyzed. Without this monitoring process it is impossible to determine whether service standards are being met and whether the standards are sufficient.

Chapter

Targeting the Upscale Client with Quality Service: The Northern Trust Approach

Our attention was drawn to Northern by an article in *Forbes* which talked about its particular brand of service. At first, what we read about was nothing out of the ordinary. Northern is a bank that claims to give good customer service. Show us a bank that doesn't! Digging further into Northern's story we found something that really caught our attention. *Northern Trust Bank is one of only four banks in the United States with fee-based income exceeding that derived from interest-related sources. In 1989 Northern's ratio was 55% fee-based versus 45% interest-based.* With a ratio like this we felt that this was a bank that had to have a pretty good insight into what customer service was all about and how to deliver it. We were right.

Quality Service Is Nothing New at Northern

Northern's recipe for customer service is both simple and complex; simple in the sense that it is deeply rooted in its culture but complex in how that culture is nurtured and cultivated. To understand how Northern developed such a client-friendly culture you first have to understand the history of Northern Trust Bank.

Northern was founded in 1889 with a capitalization of $1,000,000. Since that time it has grown into Chicago's fourth largest bank with $10.0 billion in assets and it employs more than 4,300 people. Northern's past has been characterized by a willingness to innovate and take advantage of opportunities. It was the first Chicago bank to use newspaper advertising, and they also pioneered the use of direct mail in the financial services industry.

Northern's banking philosophy is best described as conservative. This conservatism has helped the bank grow steadily since its inception even throughout the depression years when its trust assets grew from $56 million to $256 million. Throughout the decades Northern has continued its conservative approach to growth in Chicago, nationally, and internationally. In 1971 Northern acquired Security Trust Company in Miami initiating an expansion into a number of clearly identified target markets.

Shaky energy and Third World loans produced a blip in the growth chart of Northern during the 1980s. The bank responded by bringing in Mr. Weston R. Christopherson who previously served as Chairman and Chief Executive of Jewel Company, a Midwestern grocery and drugstore chain. Christopherson refocused Northern's attention onto its traditional strengths: trust and private banking. In April of 1990, Christopherson retired and shareholders elected David W. Fox, current Chairman, Chief Executive, and President.

Northern Trust Corporation, the bank's holding company, owns subsidiaries in Illinois, Arizona, California, Florida, New York, and Texas specializing in high quality fiduciary, banking, investment, and financial consulting services for individual clients as well as credit, operating, trust and advisory services for corporations, domestic and international institutions, not-for-profit organizations and public bodies. *The competitive advantage that drives this sytem and makes them different from their competitors is a dedication to the highest quality service possible.*

Northern's Strategy Links Customer Knowledge, Service, and Profits

Reliance on client service is not a new strategic option at Northern. According to Mr. Frederick H. Waddell, Senior Vice President of Strategic Planning and Corporate Marketing, it more accurately represents a refocusing on a specific strength of the bank. Northern management had always felt that quality service was a given at Northern. In 1987, Christopherson asked the critical question that launched the refocusing on quality, "Are we really delivering the level of service that we think we are?"

One reason for Northern's success is its exclusive focus on targeted markets which demand the delivery of high level service. Two such areas, trust services and private banking, are "high touch" segments with specific needs. This focus provides Northern with the luxury and ability to understand what really moves its clients. For example, while many banks are introducing cost saving technology to speed up the transaction time and reduce the cost of transactions, Northern introduces technology with a completely different philosophy. Northern incorporates technology primarily for the purpose of *enhancing the client relationship*. Saving the bank money is a secondary consideration. The emphasis is on the client and the relationship as opposed to the cost of providing the service. The customer is firmly placed in the center of its strategic approach to the market.

The linkage between superior customer service, a focused targeting effort, and profitability is clearly demonstrable in the first sentence of its mission statement:

*The mission of Northern Trust Corporation is to create
increasingly greater shareholder value by serving customers
and clients, in selected markets, in ways that meet or exceed
their expectations.*

Supporting this mission is a series of strategic corporate goals
that are designed to allow Northern to achieve its mission. These
strategic goals include the following:

1. To distinguish the Northern Trust as a financial service
   institution focused on serving selected markets with a mix
   of quality products and services where the risk-reward ratio
   is clearly in our favor.

   To achieve this longer-term goal, a number of medium-
   term goals have been set forth including:

   A. To strive constantly to determine client and customer
      needs and then match our range of capabilities and
      services with those needs to build strong, mutually-
      beneficial relationships in chosen market segments; and

   B. While it is the company's intention to be organized
      around successful profit centers based on individual
      accountability, each person who works at the Northern
      is expected to act in ways that recognize that the goals
      and well-being of the institution as a whole are superior
      to those of any individual's particular area. Individual
      effort is crucial, but teamwork across all business lines
      is an absolute requirement.

A second long-term goal speaks specifically to the issue of
customer service:

2. To inspire Northern people to excel in serving our clients
   and customers.

   A series of shorter-term goals support this goal:

   A. Never disappoint a client or customer whose expectations
      fall within the capacity of the Northern Trust to fulfill;
      indeed, to strive to anticipate and exceed those expecta-
      tions, whenever possible.

B. Unfailingly to regard those we serve or seek to serve as more important to the Northern Trust than the Northern Trust is to them: to acknowledge our clients and customers as our ultimate employers.

C. Always to conduct ourselves in ways that portray integrity, confidentiality, dignity, respect, appreciation, and professionalism; never to violate either legal or regulatory standards.

D. To be eager to solve problems and to welcome feedback on performance from those whom we serve, recognizing that open communications are the barometer of a successful business relationship.

E. Always to act in the knowledge that each individual at the Northern epitomizes the institution to our clients and customers.

Finally, the last long-term goal and its cast of supporting medium-term goals are as follows:

3. To ensure that working at the Northern is both rewarding and exciting.

A. To foster a workplace environment in which Northern people are treated with honesty, dignity, and fairness, without regard to race, creed, age, national origin, sex, or physical handicap.

B. To promote a leadership style which motivates people to be enterprising, responsive, and proud of their accomplishments and which inspires them to do their best—and then some. The style reflects two principles:

1) It is the individual and collective responsibility of Northern Trust people to serve clients and customers to their complete satisfaction.

2) The total profits produced through the efforts of Northern Trust people determine the Corporation's ability to share material rewards with its staff and shareholders and to grow.

    C. To maintain the Corporation's facilities in excellent condition so that the work environment is genuinely pleasant.

    D. To provide compensation that is fully competitive with our chosen peer group and to reward people on the basis of merit and value to the Corporation.

    E. To provide health care benefits which are competitive and which help ensure a good sense of well-being but which also recognize the individual's obligation to maintain a healthy regimen and to keep medical and hospital costs at reasonable levels.

    F. To maintain the Corporation's Thrift Incentive and Employee Stock Ownership Plans at a level which distinguishes them as the most generous in our industry, relating their rewards to the Corporation's attainment of a continuously improved net earnings.

The point in enumerating these goals is to demonstrate the clearly thought-out approach to market dominance that has made the Northern one of the more outstanding performing banks in the United States. The mission statement specifically links its philosophy of target marketing with customer service and profitability. The first long-term goal addresses the targeting concept. The medium-term goals go a step further by describing how that longer-term goal is to be achieved. Key to the achievement of this goal are the ideas of *relationship banking and teamwork*.

The second goal clearly demonstrates the Northern's recognition that high quality customer service is crucial to its success. It is not just an afterthought or a line thrown in a paragraph describing how the organization will conduct business.

The final goal and its medium-term counterparts acknowledge *the importance of treating employees the way you want the clients treated*.

These three goals manifest a management philosophy of the Northern that makes it exceptional in banking and definitely representative of some of the more enlightened business organizations in the United States. In fact, one is left with the impression that the Northern is not run like a bank but is rather *managed like a business*, a distinction that will be addressed later in more detail. One way Northern makes its idea of service work is through Signature Service.

Signature Service: Put Your Mark on Your Work!

At the heart of Northern's service philosophy and that which turns ideal to reality is Signature Service. Debra Danziger, Vice President for Marketing and Corporate Development, is the director of Signature Service and Northern's quality improvement process. Signature Service was born in 1988 as a vehicle to define outstanding service. According to Danziger, "Signature Service represents a response to the question posed by the chairman, 'Are we as good as we think we are? Are we what we are reputed to be?'" Waddell, Senior Vice President of Strategic Planning and Corporate Marketing, echoed this idea by defining Signature Service as a "corporate banner" representing this refocus on service and client orientation and "an attempt to leverage off an existing strength." Both Danziger and Waddell are quick to add that Signature Service is an evolving concept. In essence it represents an attempt to make an important and highly prized corporate value at the Northern tangible.

Waddell emphasized that Signature Service does not represent an overt action on the part of management to compete on service. "What we are trying to say is that we are a very strong service organization with a deeply ingrained culture, so let's take advantage of that strength."

Danziger added:

> Our corporate mission states that a key objective is to distinguish Northern as the outstanding financial institution within our chosen market segments. The problem is, what does outstanding mean? Signature Service is an attempt to define more precisely what our service values are. There is a further attempt for all of our business units to take the platitudes within Signature Service and make them meaningful to production staff, calling officers ... everybody in the organization.

How do you transform platitude into reality? Danziger explained:

> In a number of ways. Part of it is a definitional process. One of the platitudes is that "We are going to make it easy for you to do business with us." What does that mean? It means that we don't transfer telephone calls around this organization. It means getting it right the first time. The phrase itself can mean a variety of things to different people. Part of it gets translated into performance expectations. Part of it means communicating these values and reinforcing them constantly through messages that come out directly from the Chairman, officer meetings, annual reports, newsletters.

An important manifestation of Signature Service is the newsletter with the same title published by Northern. Figure 9-1 is a copy of the newsletter.

The newsletters contain information on a number of wide-ranging subjects. Some talk about cross-selling, how to turn problems into opportunities, how to handle complaints on the telephone, the importance of internal customers, zero defects programs, quality teams, and a host of other service-related issues. However, central to all issues of the newsletter is a portion called "From My Point of View" which allows employees throughout the organization to offer their perspectives on customer service.

For example, the head of the Customer Information Center addresses the issue of responding to dissatisfied customers. He offered the following advice to handling customer complaints:

> Listen and let the customer talk. If the banker takes a defensive position with the customer, nothing is accomplished. We have a tendency to interpret the customer's use of 'you' as meaning us individually rather than the bank. If we allow the customer to air his problems, we can intercede and sort through the situation. Every customer problem or complaint is an opportunity to make something positive.

Figure 9-1
Signature Service Newsletter

Signature Service
Put your
mark on your work!

June, 1990

Food For Thought

This issue of Signature Service is filled with various articles based on books, studies and other materials published in the customer service newsletter, **Front-line Service**.

As we continue in our efforts to provide excellent service to our clients and to one another, you may find it helpful to take a moment for some tips and advice.

The information may be new or it may be a reminder of some basic techniques which, when thoroughly carried out, could mean the difference between winning over or losing a valued client.

Advice About Good Listening

Logically, about half of the total time you spend communicating is devoted to listening. Unfortunately, that's often the side of the process many people take for granted. They concentrate hard on what they're saying, but slack off when listening, which can waste time, anger others, affect productivity, and hurt an individual's reputation or that of a company.

To improve listening skills, work on these good listening habits:

1. **Develop powers of concentration.** Learn to ignore distractions.

2. **Find something of interest in the information.** You can find areas of interest in most any message.

3. **Overlook speakers' mannerisms.** Don't prejudge the value of a message due to a speaker's delivery or appearance.

4. **Focus on central ideas.** Identify the major points of a message.

5. **Hold your fire.** Separate the tasks of interpreting and evaluating messages.

6. **Work at listening.** Realize that listening entails work, not relaxation.

7. **Pay attention to body language.** Visual cues can help accurately interpret the meaning of a person's works.

8. **Capitalize on thought speed.** Use thought speed to mentally summarize information, anticipate the next point, and listen between the lines to the tone of voice.

9. **Paraphrase remarks.** Summarize a point back to the speaker to check understanding and seek feedback.

Flights Of Anger Can Be Piloted

Angry customers take emotional flights in venting their frustrations that always have a beginning, a peak, and an end -- and can be managed if understood, according to Ralph W. and Victoria J. Dacy, Dacy Training and Communications, El Toro, California, writing in their booklet, How to Avoid

Conflict with an Angry Customer.

A normal flight, the authors say, will usually run its course within seconds or minutes if a customer is "left alone" in an emotional outburst. "When you listen reflectively and ask questions about the real problem,

there is a dampening effect. Ask a question and your customer feels compelled to answer. When your question is problem related, your customer will realize you are interested in helping solve the problem. This will cut the flight low and short and the customer will quickly become rational."

Figure 9-1
Signature Service Newsletter *continued*

A Sense Of Humor Is Required

Everyone knows how valuable a sense of humor is in dealing with customers. But sometimes we need to be reminded because the ability to see the light side of life is often the first thing to disappear when we get caught up in **doing what has to be done!** Jeanne Robertson, a keynote speaker at the International Customer Service Association conference in Nashville, told attendees, "If you use humor -- not comedy -- on a daily basis, it can be one of the most valuable tools in customer service. Unfortunately, we've been so tuned into stand-up comedy that people think having a sense of humor means being funny."

But having a sense of humor, Robertson says, has nothing to do with being funny. "It has a lot to do with being able to laugh at yourself and to accept things you can't change. If we are going to use humor as part of our strategies for success, we have to see humor in stressful situations and make the most of them. In tense situations some people get sky high. Some people fall apart. Then there are those people who see the humor, make the most of it, and figure out what it means later."

Attitude Is Critical

How important to your company is your attitude with customers? Important enough that you could drive away almost three out of every four people if you make the wrong impression, according to Original Research Corp, II, a Chicago firm that does follow-up calls to six million customers a year for car dealers and other service companies.

Almost 70 percent of the people surveyed by Original Research say they have decided not to go back to a place of business because it seemed the employees didn't care about them or their own work.

"The overriding message we tell our frontline people is that customers don't care how much you know until they know how much you care," says Howard Tullman, president of Original Research. The company coaches people in three areas for good customer service: **Courtesy** (friendly and respectful), **Style** (efficient, responsive, and knowledgeable), and **Attitude** (concerned, helpful, and interested). "The front line is where the battle is won or lost," says Tullman.

A recent Gallup poll supports that sentiment: consumers rated courteous, polite treatment as the top factor in determining the quality of service they receive.

Star Quality

What does it take to provide "star quality" customer service? A checklist created by Development Dimensions International (Pittsburgh, PA) to be used by managers in selecting service-oriented employees is a good set of guidelines for knowing what customers -- and employers -- expect of you on the front line:

- Customer Sensitivity
- Energy
- Impact
- Initiative
- Motivation to Serve Customers
- Oral Communication
- Persuasiveness/Sales Ability
- Resilience
- Situation Analysis/ Judgment
- Technical Knowledge
- Work Standards

"Signature Service, Put Your Mark on Your Work," June 1990.

The manager of the Research Services Group addressed the role of research in reinforcing client service commitment by saying:

> Often when we think of what makes good customer service, we simply say, "I'll know it when I see it." Our job is to define quality by measuring how our clients perceive the services we are providing them. In this way, we can better capitalize on Northern's strong reputation for quality customer service.

A Vice President from one of the support areas added the following point of view:

> The commitment of quality service by our support staff is no less important to Northern's goals. Whether in recruiting a new hire, moving computer terminals, transporting packages, processing a check, or typing a new piece of business, the bank relies on support staff to help them perform their jobs better. This ultimately enables Northern to provide superior service to our clients. Northern people deserve the same service as our outside clients and we have the obligation to provide it.

The different topics addressed in each newsletter make Danziger's point about the evolving nature of service and the continual attempt to define it even more cogent. Signature Service provides all employees with the opportunity to take a basic, but quintessential value like service and define it in the way that impacts their job in the different business units that comprise the corporation. It is in this way that a number of platitudes are translated into reality.

Signature Service Council Drives Signature Service

The driving force behind Signature Service is the Signature Service Council, a group comprised of senior and executive managers from all the major business units and support areas. The Council meets at least once a month attesting to the idea that at the Northern, service is a process not a program.

The Council is chaired by Waddell and Danziger. Waddell explained the purpose of the Council:

> We are a fairly far-flung operation with a broad set of experiences. The Signature Service Council brings people together from all major client and support groups to work on issues. We come together to share and learn, that is, to understand those things we are doing quite well that we might be able to implement elsewhere. Likewise, when an area is having problems, we try to surface those issues. We buy services from each other. So, it's important to learn how we affect each other.

Danziger further explained the mission of the Council:

> The purpose of the Council is to reinforce the concept of Signature Service to the corporation. In this regard we have been very successful. You can talk to anyone around here and they know the term "Signature Service." Beyond that, we wanted to promote the idea that quality service is not a program but a process. Therefore, we adopted a threefold mission. The first is visionary in nature; to take the concept of Signature Service and translate it into something meaningful, actionable, and measurable to the different business units.
>
> The second mission is one of communication; to keep finding ways to reinforce the message internally but also to find ways to take the message to our clients.
>
> The third aspect of the Council is to focus on quality. The idea of quality has been elusive. This has turned out to be the main focus of the Council; to find ways to define, deliver and measure the level of quality that is appropriate for this organization. To that end Northern has created a quality template and currently is assessing the level of quality throughout the corporation.

Teamwork and Relationship Banking Go Hand-in-Hand

The importance of teamwork at the Northern is a critical factor in its considerable success. The following is an example of how Northern teamwork has overcome a typically territorial problem encountered in many banks. Discount brokerage has been offered by the Northern since 1984. However, in late 1989, management decided to expand their services in this area by offering full service brokerage to their clients. Full service brokerage was generated from research findings indicating that a significant number of high-net-worth individuals had a full-service broker relationship and were active managers of their own portfolios.

A goal of 1,500 accounts was set for 1990. To date, Northern has far exceeded this goal by opening 6,000 accounts representing $230 million in cash and securities.

What is interesting about this new service is the origin of these accounts. According to James Anderson, president of Northern Trust Brokerage, almost 60% of the accounts represent upgrades from the discount services, resulting from a direct mail campaign to current discount brokerage customers. *However, in the first six months of operations about 55% of the clients were referrals from bank personnel, including institutional clients referred from Trust.*

This referral demonstrates the kind of teamwork at the Northern which makes it possible to give clients the service that keeps them loyal and satisfied. Brokerage agreed from the start to open up its books for the Trust Department, twice a year, to identify candidates for trust services. It also speaks to the internalization of corporate goals concerning teamwork. One of the Northern's goals specifically addressed the idea of teamwork: "Individual effort is crucial; but teamwork across all business lines is an absolute requirement."

The success with the introduction of the brokerage service also recognizes the importance of cross-selling at the Northern and one other concept that is at the heart of their commitment to clients—relationship banking. At the Northern, customers are referred to as clients for a specific purpose. *The Northern is a relationship bank, not a transactional bank. Northern personnel think in terms of clients instead of customers because the former captures the idea of relationships, while the latter is more descriptive of a transaction orientation.*

The Northern Cares for its People

Northern firmly believes in the idea that you treat your employees the way you want the employee to treat the customer. Perhaps one of the Northern's greatest assets is the loyalty of its people. It is this loyalty that helps make Northern service outstanding. Figure 9-2 is a copy of a letter from a customer sent to Northern's Chairman and President, David Fox.

This is just one example of the kind of customer service a customer can expect at Northern. The level of service demonstrated from the guard at Northern makes it unique in an intensively competitive financial services market.

Northern uses a variety of reward systems that make employees realize the importance of their contribution to the overall success of the organization. For example, one incentive program ties an employee's remuneration to three levels of performance. The largest portion, about 50%, is tied to the performance of the Northern Trust Company. The second largest portion is directly related to the employee's business unit's performance, while the smallest portion is directly based on the individual's performance. This type of reward system goes a long way to fostering teamwork across the different business units.

An Employee Stock Ownership Plan was created in 1989. Over the next 10 years, 1.5 million shares of Northern Trust stock will be distributed to employees. Northern people participate in a generous 401-k plan that matches an employee's contribution by as much as 125%, based on the corporation's realization of established earnings targets. A significant portion of the assets of this plan is in the form of stock, which, when combined with the stock held in the ESOP, according to Waddell, "gives Northern employees about a 20% ownership in the Northern."

In addition, there are a number of other employee programs designed to incent exceptional service performance. The Staff Recognition Award program pays between $250 and $10,000 for outstanding performance on the part of an employee. The need to recognize the employee's daily victories gave rise to the Signature Service Spirit Program, a nonmonetary recognition program that publicly acknowledges employee contributions.

Figure 9-2
Letter from a Customer

April 13, 1990

Mr. David W. Fox
Chairman and President
Northern Trust Bank

Dear Mr. Fox:

I have had a checking and business account with the Northern Trust Bank since 1979. Normally, I come to Northern Trust in mid-day to do my banking. However, on April 2, I came to the bank at 5:15 PM to cash a check. I was completely out of money. When I got there, to my surprise, there were no tellers to cash my check.

I met a bank guard who told me that the bank teller services now close at 4 PM. I explained that I had no money and that I did not have a check-cashing card. I told him that I didn't even have the money to buy myself a train ticket home. He asked me how much a train ticket would cost and I told him $3. He then gave me $5 out of his pocket. He did not even ask me my name when he gave me the money.

You are very fortunate to have such an employee. Your customers will never leave Northern Trust with people like him around.

Very truly yours,

A Very Satisfied Customer

Northern has a strong reputation for taking care of its employees. The bank offers its employees a subsidized cafeteria, an on-site day-care center, gym, and an indoor parking facility. This is an expensive proposition but evidently well worth it. According to Chairman Fox, "It's too expensive not to take care of your employees."

Bottom-lining the Northern Approach

There is little doubt that the Northern is doing something right. In 1989, ROA for Northern Trust was 1.08% with a reported return on equity of 24%. These numbers placed Northern Trust in the top 11 of the 100 largest banks in the U.S., even though it ranks only 52nd in asset size!

A key component in its success is its devotion to high quality service and a deep abiding belief that it is the high level of service that differentiates it in the marketplace. There are several valuable lessons to be learned from the Northern.

First, Northern Trust has a deeply rooted culture based on high quality service. This is not a new strategic option. Rather, it is an attempt to leverage off an existing strength. However, it is not content to live off a reputation. Instead, customer service is nurtured and developed as a critical cultural value. In talking with several Northern employees about their jobs, what you consistently hear is, "The client is the most important part of my job." When asked what makes the Northern different from other financial institutions, they responded, "The level of service we give."

What is interesting about this is that the Northern does not invest extensively in hours of classroom training in customer service. Much of its training is on-the-job. New hires are sent a letter from the chairman before they report to work talking about the importance of Signature Service. During the first six weeks of employment they attend a "welcome" conducted by the chairman who again talks about service and its importance at the Northern. But the greatest training and the greatest emphasis come from their fellow workers. Experienced employees become role models for newer employees and pass on the service ethic.

Perhaps the most important mentor is the CEO. Waddell related a story told by David Fox (CEO) in a management meeting.

> Dave received a letter from one of Northern's employees. In the letter, the employee recounts an episode when David was walking across the lobby and saw a discarded deposit ticket on the floor. He bent down, picked it up, and threw it in the waste basket. The employee went on to say "I saw you do this and I can only say that if that is the degree of commitment that you have made to quality at Northern Trust I hope I can live up to that same commitment."

According to Waddell, Fox was not only touched but was amazed at the response to the little action he took. These values run throughout the organization down to the service reps. Feedback letters from customers acknowledge the high level of service and the demonstrable sense of caring that Northern employees show.

Anna Quinlan runs the Demand Account Services Organization at Northern Trust. She is responsible for getting out about 200,000 DDA statements a month. Quality is a big part of her job with about 28% of her performance expectations linked to quality. Quinlan is responsive to a number of quality standards designed to help her organization reach a zero defects level. The worst month was 400 errors while the best was 32. "Out of about 200,000 statements handled a month that's not too bad. But it's not good enough," she adds.

Another important aspect of the Northern brand of service is management concern for the employees of Northern Trust. Northern Trust has always considered itself on the cutting edge of employee benefits. This has evidently paid dividends for the organization. Northern links employee remuneration with, not only individual performance, but to unit and corporate performance. In so doing, it is easier for the employee to understand the "big picture" and to understand their role in the delivery of quality service. Even if they are serving internal employees instead of external employees, this compensation picture socks home the idea that everyone has a role in client service.

The Northern is a caring organization. It believes that to get the level of service necessary to support its position in the market, it has to make sure that its employees are well cared for. This inspires a loyalty and puts into motion the "cycle of good service" discussed in Chapter 1.

Finally, the Northern Trust is run like a business. When you talk with its management you get the impression you are talking with the corporate staff at IBM, Ford Motors, or some other business, and not a bank. The distinction is difficult to articulate but is manifested in a solid planning approach with well articulated goals and objectives, standards to govern results, and control systems to determine whether objectives are being met. It is an approach to banking that is very business-like and extremely professional. It relies more heavily on a structured management system as opposed to the individual charisma of an individual or an informal management system.

Chapter

Customer Service Lessons from Four Outstanding Warriors

You have just finished reading about four different banks in four different parts of the country using top notch customer service to accomplish four different strategies. As different as the strategic positions and managements may be, there are a number of characteristics common to all four excellent programs. In this last chapter we will examine some of the elements of each strategy which we think are common across all of the banks. These ten lessons are the essence of what makes these four banks so outstanding.

Lesson 1: "Before You Can Make a Great Dream Come True, You First Have to Have a Great Dream."

This is a particularly important lesson for those managements contemplating switching to customer service as a strategic option. You will recall from the discussion of Seafirst Bank, Luke Helms had a solid picture or a model of how Seafirst would compete. His overall blueprint was McDonald's, with added components from Nordstroms and other successful retailers. His vision of banking at Seafirst revolved around the idea of independently managed franchises where headquarters provided support services. To make this dream come true Helms needed to view his business not from the traditional perspective of banking, but rather from a more radical but contemporary perspective of retailing. As Helms said, "We suddenly realized that we had 180 retail businesses and that we were in the retailing business!"

This vision began with a hard and thorough analysis of what his current competitive position was and should be. If retail banking was to be the way in which Seafirst was to be positioned, then Helms was going to fashion it after one of the most successful retailers in the country. This adherence to a clear and focused vision has guided much of the decision making at Seafirst. Indeed, it goes beyond the current situation. Helms delights in talking about the idea of selling branches as franchises and letting the individual franchises run themselves, much like McDonald's currently does.

Helms supports his vision of Seafirst banking from the bottom up. His development of Seafirst College (patterned after Hamburger U at McDonald's) is designed to equip his management with the tools and skills necessary to run the organization according to the blueprint of his vision.

Griffin Norquist, at the Bank of Yazoo City, likewise explains the genesis of his strategic shift in terms of a vision of what his bank needed to be to compete in his market. His "Wal-Mart

Theory of Banking" contains an explicit model of how a smaller community bank must compete against a much larger, well-run bank. His desire and drive to make the Bank of Yazoo City the model of customer service in the market area is paying strong dividends.

Northern Trust's vision is readily discernible in its comprehensive strategic plan. There is little doubt as to the type of organization that Northern trust has chosen to be. It is a well thought out and extremely well implemented strategy. Moreover, as both Frederick Waddell and Debra Danziger indicated, Northern's vision of customer service is well communicated throughout the organization. This is apparent from conversations with Northern personnel.

It is difficult to talk about a vision without discussing one of the most important functions of a CEO. From our own experience in the banking industry, we have encountered many top executives who are more *reactive* than vision oriented. They lack the clear picture of what the bank should be and equally important, how the bank will get there. The operational pressures of day-to-day duties and obligations tend to limit top management vision and force a more short-term orientation. Most of the CEOs and top management people we spoke with told us how difficult it was to develop this longer-term orientation. Each one, however, told us how important that vision was.

What are some keys for turning a vision into a reality? The first is that the CEO must be committed to the vision. He or she must believe in the future state for his or her organization and marshal all the necessary resources at his or her command to transform the vision into a reality. There can be no qualification or hesitation at committing the necessary resources to accomplish the vision.

Equally important, the CEO must be willing to stay on the course. There will be a number of competing forces and activities arguing for a reallocation of effort and resources. The temptation is to divert those efforts and resources into what may appear to be more important programs or courses of action. There is no quick fix for transforming a strategic vision into a corporate reality.

Supporting this effort is essential. The people that surround Luke Helms, Griffin Norquist, or David Fox are all committed to the idea of top notch customer service and will do whatever is necessary to make sure their bank delivers it. If you ask these people what is the most important part of their job, they will tell you making sure that their customers are taken care of in a way that makes their bank stand out from the rest.

Several top executives told us that from time to time they wondered if they had committed the bank to the right course. There is always a potential for doubt in a situation of this magnitude. All, however, did indicate that they were committed to making their bank the top bank in the market. After all, as Luke Helms pointed out, "How can you go wrong giving your customers outstanding service?"

Lesson 2: "When The CEO Eats, Sleeps, and Above all Sweats Customer Service, Others Will Follow."

Richard Starman, former director of corporate communications at McDonald's, recounts the times when Ray Kroc would travel from store to store, park the car in the parking lot and begin to pick up loose paper and debris that were in the lot. Pretty soon the employees in the store would look out the window and wonder who that fellow was. You can imagine their surprise when they found out that the man with the fanatical concern for cleanliness was none other than Ray Kroc.

This is what the top executives meant when they told us that customer service begins at the top. More customer service initiatives have failed because the CEO became excited about customer service one day and abandoned it shortly after for "other activities more important." This is a sure fire prescription for failure.

Tom Hawker, Griffin Norquist, Luke Helms, and David Fox all sweat customer service. Their commitment to the idea of providing outstanding customer service is made manifest in daily activities by these top executives. Norquist attended all the training sessions, the same ones that his tellers attended. David Fox never lets an opportunity pass for communicating the importance of customer service to his people or demonstrating that he is not too important to bend down and pick up a piece of paper in the lobby. Tom Hawker is a customer service leader. His very actions set standards for the rest of his people.

There are any number of ways of demonstrating this commitment. As we mentioned earlier, Griffin Norquist spent numerous hours in customer service training sessions with the rest of his employees. This made a big impact on the people. There was no doubt in their minds that customer service was going to be an important part of the way they did business at the Bank of Yazoo City. Tom Hawker is always on the floor with customers who need service. While some of his other work may suffer from inattention, his customers will not. In fact, during the heady growth of Concord Commercial, Tom has been urged to move his office to a nonbanking floor. He has resisted moving because it takes him away from the customers and doesn't allow him to demonstrate the importance of customer service to the other employees.

Luke Helms, on the other hand, cannot be on the floor of over 180 branches. Instead his commitment is demonstrated through the development of a position charged with assuring the delivery of top notch customer service. He has spent millions of dollars on transforming Seafirst into the market's most outstanding provider of customer service. In addition, his daily trips to the branches and his constant preaching about customer service continually reinforce its importance.

The issue of leadership is an important one. The kinds of service that are required to make an organization like Northern Trust or any of the other banks such outstanding examples of customer service can not be managed. It's not possible to manage the behaviors of all employees to that extent. What you see in these examples of outstanding service are people who have bought the idea of providing outstanding customer service into the bank. A powerful part of the selling effort is the leadership qualities of the top executives.

Delegating this aspect of the process sends a negative message to the employees. One employee explained, "We can tell if something is important in our bank if the president is actively involved in it. If he isn't, all you have to do is keep your head down for a couple of weeks and it will pass by." One employee in a bank where the customer service strategy never got off the ground told us something very revealing about her bank. She said that when the CEO announced their new strategy, everyone referred to it as "just another one of the flavors of the month." This attitude reflects a lack of commitment on management's part and is indicative of an organization without a sure and steady hand on the corporate helm. *Customer service is too important to be just anther flavor of the month. It is up to the top executive to make sure that customer service becomes a corporate passion, the driving force in the bank.*

Lesson 3: "One of the Hardest Things I Have Had to Do Was Give Up Control."

This was a confession of Griffin Norquist but was a sentiment that was echoed by all of the top executives and managers. *To make a customer service strategy work, really work, decision making has to be pushed down the organizational chart to where the service is actually delivered. All of these organizations have empowered their employees to give high quality service. Management does not get in the way of service delivery.*

Luke Helms understands the need to empower employees with both skills and responsibility. He has established, in conjunction with the University of Washington, Seafirst College, where his managers go through extensive training on "How to Run a Franchise." To date he has sent more than 500 of his people through this program. In addition, he goes to great lengths to keep his people from headquarters out of the day-to-day functioning of the branches. He is a firm believer in the idea of letting service happen where it happens—at the customer level.

All of the top executives in the banks that we studied have gone so far as to empower their front line people to make corrections up to various amounts of money. Angry customers who have been charged for various situations can appeal to the teller and get an immediate response if the situation involves less than a certain amount. The rationale for this approach? Helms points out that once the complaint is brought to his attention he will make sure the customer is taken care of anyway. Why should that person have to wait for the inevitable?

This same thinking has caused Griffin Norquist to invert his organizational chart and put the customer on top. Norquist is developing a culture in the Bank of Yazoo City wherein the customer drives the bank. In order to do this he has realized that the old authoritarian type of management system still flourishing in many banks will not work. Customer service occurs on the front line. His job is to make sure that the front line people are prepared to deliver it. He works to remove all impediments that might lessen the service that those people can deliver.

All of these banks hold a strong belief in giving the people the skills and knowledge to do their jobs better than anyone else. This is an important aspect of their success. The people at these banks are constantly learning how to deliver that high quality service that makes their banks stand out from the others in the market. This is a must because there is no ceiling to the level of customer service that a bank offers its market. In order to satisfy this dynamic and insatiable demand for service, outstanding banks must constantly provide their people with the means to do so.

How do you know when you can trust your employees with their newly empowered status? All top executives reported it was a trial and error process. Some were afraid that the employees would give the bank away. However, instead of giving away the bank, the employees had to be pushed to rectify problems with reimbursements. So for those executives who are afraid of letting their employees smooth over customer complaints with refunds or reimbursements—relax. The likelihood is that your employees will be a stingy as you would be, maybe even more so.

Lesson 4: "You Can't Manage What You Can't Measure."

All the banks in our study spent a significant amount of time, dollars, and effort in monitoring their service levels. This is an essential ingredient in the success of their programs.

The Bank of Yazoo City began its implementation of a customer service strategy with an initial benchmark study of their current level of customer service. The Northern Trust and Seafirst systematically monitor changes in the perceived level of customer service. This monitoring is designed to identify the strengths and weaknesses of their service delivery systems. It is not used in a punitive manner.

In *Winning Banks* we presented a questionnaire which captures many of the same elements that are used by the different banks in this book. Our approach for measuring service quality goes beyond a simple evaluative purpose and includes a means of identifying those service dimensions which are most responsible for explaining a customer's overall perception of service and their willingness to recommend the bank to a friend. This aspect of the questionnaire is very important because it builds upon the credibility of individual word of mouth, as pointed out in Chapter 1.

The banks in our study tend to rely on periodical measures of customer perceptions. This allows them to manage those aspects of the delivery system in which they feel they might be deficient. Moreover, several of the banks use different measuring techniques. While most rely on survey methodologies, several of the banks also hire independent shopping services as part of the monitoring process. Another technique that is often mentioned is the use of focus groups. These groups can make the measurement of service perceptions more affordable to smaller banks. While there might be a tradeoff between the statistical nature of a survey and the more exploratory nature of the focus group, the latter can provide insightful information.

Frequent measures are important for another reason. The probabilistic nature of the survey approach suggests that what is more important than the single "snapshot" of service perceptions is the trend of perceptions. Statistical theory accommodates the possibility of deviant measures. That is, a one-time measure may not reflect the "true" level of perceived service. Multiple measures, taken over time, tend to discount this potential deviation and give management a more realistic idea of the actual perceptions of its customers. One source of data measured at one point in time can not capture the complexity of the service relationship of the bank with the customer.

Multiple measures would have been helpful to some of our client banks that have actually missed the point in the measuring process. Several of our clients have been content with a single measure of their service level. Management reviews the numbers and says, "Everything looks okay. We don't need to do any more surveys." Implicit in this response is that customer service is a static dimension of bank performance and not a dynamic dimension. Moreover, management seldom uses this information as a means for managing this crucial element of the bank's strategic output. When the information is good, management tends to view it as corroborative in nature, evoking a "That's what I thought" type of response. Some of our clients have actually discounted the bad news. Instead of using the surveys as a means of managing the potential problem, they have rather tended to blame the survey for "obviously erroneous information." This misuse of the measurement process is usually found in those banks in which Lessons 1 and 2 have been ignored.

One final point should be made concerning the measurement process. Many banks want to compare themselves to other banks to determine the relative quality of their service offering. This is a spurious comparison. The actual comparison should be against some of the more outstanding *businesses* in the market area. Banks are not setting service standards and expectations. At best, most of them are responding to them. As we pointed out in Chapter 1, customers' expectations are being determined by nonbank organizations. It is against these types of organizations that a bank's service quality should be compared.

Lesson 5: "We Must Focus on What We Can Do for the Customer, Not What We Can't."

A teller at Seafirst bank made this lesson apparent to us. When we asked her what was the most important part of her job she said, "We must focus on what we can do for the customer, not what we can't." It is exactly this attitude that explains why Rey at Seafirst would unhesitatingly help a customer change a flat tire or open his locked car. It is this idea that drives Holly to deliver papers to a customer when this task is not included in her job description. It is this notion of customer service that makes a bank guard at Northern Trust give a customer train fare or a Vice President at the Bank of Yazoo City help farmers haul cotton at midnight.

This attitude is indicative of a culture that focuses on the customer. It is a manifestation of the importance of customer service to that bank. It is the result of top executives who have had great dreams and are committed to making those dreams come true.

In our experience with banks that have been unsuccessful in the development of a viable customer service strategy, this attitude is missing. In these types of banks, instead of focusing on what they can do for the customer, we find the operating dictum is more neatly captured by the idea, "What can we do for ourselves." This attitude closes banks from 1:00 to 2:30 in the afternoon, ostensibly to "balance the books." This attitude keeps banks closed until 9:00 in the morning and keeps them closed on Saturday. Driving these decisions are any number of "reasons" why the banks can not accommodate these changes. However, reading between the lines is the one real reason, "it's not convenient for the bank."

This is not the attitude of the management and the employees of the banks we have included in this book. Tom Hawker encourages a single-minded focus on the customer. It explains why the sign on his door reads "Hours: 9:00 AM to 4:00 AM— Other Times By Appointment." It also explains why employees will open the bank after closing times to help customers. Every suggestion for improving customer service is examined for its impact on the customer, not the bank employee. It is this type of thinking that developed his highly successful courier service that we discussed in the chapter on Concord Bank. It is this type of attitude that governs the use of technology at Northern Trust. Technology is evaluated for its impact on customer service, in addition to its cost implications.

A significant aspect of this focus is the training that these banks provide their employees and the level of empowerment given them. The training provides them with the know-how and the empowerment lets them exercise that know-how. This combination enables bank employees to begin to see banking, not from the banking side of the business but rather from the customer side of the business. This empathy helps generate additional, innovative ways of serving the customers. Supportive of this "intrapreneurial" focus is a management that encourages this type of behavior. You don't find these managements saying, "That's nice but it's not really your job to worry about those things." In these banks it's everybody's job to think about the customer, not just management's.

Lesson 6: "It's Not a Bank, It's Like a Home for Our Customers."

Perhaps nowhere was this lesson made so manifest than at Concord Commercial Bank. Upon our arrival we were invited to attend a weekly meeting of the bank in which Tom Hawker discussed everything from upcoming parties to the bank's financial condition. The atmosphere in the bank radiated a sense of family, a sense that everyone was working together to accomplish one thing—to give the customers the best service that they could get. This sense of teamwork and family was transferred directly to the customer. Customers of Concord Commercial Bank felt as if they were a significant and important part of the bank. In fact, we chose Concord Commercial as one of our outstanding banks because of the tremendous positive response given by its customers when we were researching our first book,

Winning Banks. During focus group sessions with Concord's customers we were hard pressed to find anything that they did not like about the bank, its people, and the way they treated their customers. Concord made its customers feel as if they were part of a family.

This is an important point. While many banks pride themselves on friendly courteous service, Concord has been able to create a strong culture that goes beyond smiling and saying "thank you." The feeling that customers receive from Concord is that the bank is actually there to help them, not to simply make money from their patronage. It is evident in the willingness of bank personnel to stay late to help customers, to open the doors of the bank after it has officially closed, to go out to the business site and help the customer, and of course, in the genuine concern that Tom Hawker expresses for the customers.

Many banks fail in instilling this type of culture because top management fails to heed Lessons one and two. Instead, top management writes a memo saying that everyone in the bank is going to be friendly and give good customer service. It just doesn't work that way.

Many would argue that this is a small bank phenomenon and that this type of culture is a lot more difficult to manage in a larger institution. That is probably true but it can still be done. Seafirst Bank in Seattle does it and does it well. The 180 branches at Seafirst exude this sense of welcome and willingness to serve the customer. You will recall the stories about Rey and Holly and their genuine love of helping customers. This type of attitude pervades the entire Seafirst system.

Northern Trust also has been very successful in inoculating this sense of family to its employees. One example is the willingness of the bank guard to lend a customer train money.

The Bank of Yazoo City depends heavily on this element to compete against much larger institutions. Vice Presidents hauling cotton for farmers at midnight is a good indication of the kind of commitment they have to treating customers as part of the family.

All of these banks have gone the extra customer service mile in creating a culture and an atmosphere that supports their outstanding reputations as top notch customer service deliverers. The people in the bank are more than simply courteous and friendly. They really care about their customers and their customers know it. This is not a culture that can be created overnight. It is not an atmosphere that can be installed automatically by bringing in some motivational speaker for a one hour burst of enthusiasm. It is the result of hard work and a commitment to the idea that their bank is going to be the best deliverer of customer service in their market area.

Lesson 7: "Treat Your Employees the Way You Want Your Customers Treated."

This lesson was taught to us by a woman at Seafirst Bank. She reduced a complicated relationship between employees and customer service to the idea that employees will treat their customers the way they are treated. What we have seen in all the banks that we have recognized as outstanding customer service banks is their recognition that the employee is more than a mere unit of production. Tellers are more than robots hired to count money and make transactions. In the outstanding banks that we have studied, people are valued workers who contribute to the overall success of the operation. They are valued for much more than their mere ability to perform a task ennumerated on their job description. They are valued for their creativity, their intellect, and their problem-solving abilities.

Remember the solution the employees came up with at the Bank of Yazoo City? Norquist increased customer service and reduced costs by listening to what his employees had to say about a problem. Implicit in this action is a realization on the CEO's part that his employees could contribute more to the successful operation of the organization than the mere completion of tasks outlined in their job descriptions could.

Most personnel directors will claim that their bank treats their employees in this same manner. But, to get a different and perhaps more accurate view of the relative worth of employees, all you have to do is listen to other bank executives talk. "She's just a teller. You have to spell everything out for her!" "We could never get our people to do that." These, unfortunately, are typical of the comments we have heard from people in a number of banks that have wanted to compete on a customer service basis. The probability of success is greatly diminished with attitudes like this.

Not only does management expound these types of attitudes, management should hear what the employees think of their "leaders." It is not surprising to find a mutual lack of respect. Given this destructive atmosphere, it's no small wonder that customers are driven from the bank. Attitudes like this are not present in the outstanding banks that we studied. On the contrary, management recognized that the strength of the bank was the people who worked in the bank.

The Bank of Yazoo City is notable in this instance because it had to recreate an atmosphere of trust and a sense of team that was damaged by some necessary structural and strategic changes. Griffin Norquist has focused much attention and effort on creating an atmosphere of trust and communication throughout the bank. Without this sense of teamwork, bank employees have little chance of giving customers the kind of treatment that would make the bank stand out as tops in its market. Does it work? Just ask the employees. While some problems still exist, virtually all employees talk about what a great place the Bank of Yazoo City is to work for and how the atmosphere and culture created by Griffin Norquist makes it easy for them to *want* to give their customers the best service they can.

The situation at Northern Trust is somewhat different. This bank has a legacy of treating its employees very well. They are noted for many personnel innovations in banking and having created an atmosphere of trust, respect, and teamwork. In fact, our conversations with employees of Northern Trust clearly demonstrate the validity of the cyclical relationship between employee treatment and customer satisfaction. All employees praised their working conditions and their treatment at the bank.

Several indicated that many of their friends would welcome the opportunity to work at the bank.

The story at Seafirst and Concord is the same. At Seafirst, many of the branch personnel told us of the quality of their working conditions and how they felt those conditions made it so much easier to treat the customer with special consideration. At Concord, Tom Hawker's open management style communicates a caring and a respect for all employees. These values are often repeated when employees describe their job.

Lesson 8: "What You Stroke Is What You Get."

Too often bank managements preach one thing and then reward something else. At year end these same managements are left wondering what went wrong. People will act in their best interests. When those interests are aligned with the interests of the organization, things get done. When they are not, things don't get done. In other words, if customer service is to be a valued strategic output of the organization, make sure that customer service gets rewarded!

This point was brought home to us at one of our client banks. Customer service was to be the new strategic thrust. Management preached customer service at every opportunity. At the end of the year a survey indicated not only did customers *not* see an improvement in service levels, but a significant portion felt service had declined. When we asked how the bank employees were rewarded for their service effort, the CEO said no reward system was necessary. It was expected that people would do what they were told. They were also told to cut costs and cross-sell services. Moreover, no customer service performance appraisal was conducted. Small wonder that customers saw little changes or even negative changes in the level of service they received.

All of the banks that are described in this book make a strong overt effort to reward outstanding examples of customer service. Special incentive plans, dinners, medals, pins, pats on the back, recognition, monetary rewards, and "a job well done" are used by all the banks. Some of these programs have been more successful than others. However, key to their successful implementation is an understanding of what is important to the employees.

What is remarkable about the incentive systems, either formal or informal, is that these people do not behave in a Pavlovian manner. In these excellent banks, customer service is such a fundamental part of the culture that employees go out of their way to give their customers great service. The incentives draw employee attention to the importance of customer service and become a motivational means for developing the necessary attitudes and resultant behavior to support the strategy.

What is obvious in these banks is that no one is standing over an employee's shoulder making them deliver high quality customer service. In other words, bank employees are providing this high quality service with a minimal amount of supervision. What makes this work in these banks is that these managements have been successful in selling an idea, the idea of customer service. How do you get a guy like Rey to change a customer's flat tire? How do you get someone like Holly to take it upon herself to take a set of papers to a customer? How do you get a vice president of a bank to help a customer haul cotton at midnight? How do you get a bank guard to loan a customer train fare? The answer is that there is very little management and supervision of these behaviors. These individuals have bought into the idea that providing customers with the highest level of customer service is a crucial element of their job. They believe in it as a way of business.

An important part of this selling process is the leadership roles provided by top management. Tom Hawker is an outstanding example. Ask his employees why they do some things and they will tell you that they have seen Hawker do them. The same is true for Griffin Norquist or David Fox. Leadership is an integral part of the process. Stroking the proper kinds of behavior supports the process.

The Northern Trust process incorporates performance expectations regarding customer service. Employees meet with their department heads and outline their expectations regarding various aspects of performance, including customer service. At the end of the evaluation period they are held accountable for their performance. The key is that these employees set their own levels of expectation, levels that are determined not only by potential rewards but by a culture that prides itself in this type of behavior.

Lesson 9: "Customer Service Is Our Business, Our Only Business."

This lesson may be reminiscent of the old Gerber pledge "Babies are our business, our only business." What this means is that those organizations that believe customer service is their only business are the organizations that have a very focused orientation as to what they are and why they are in business. Many banks have managed themselves into a commodity position. They and their product/service offering are seen as undifferentiated; their services are by their own design, highly substitutable, and the only way they compete is on a price basis.

The banks described in this book don't operate that way. These are banks that understand that what brings customers to their bank is the exceptional high service standards and the equally high levels of customer service that the bank actually delivers. Luke Helms at Seafirst probably understands this better than most bank executives. His charge, you may recall, was "Get good at something, quick!" He realized that retail banking was the way to go and once he decided on the market position, the specific strategy became equally apparent. If you are going to become a retailer you have to give your customers the highest level of service possible. By focusing on high quality service, the banking side of the business will take care of itself. Customers will come to your bank not for products that they can get at any bank but for the attention and service that only your bank can deliver.

People choose to bank at Concord Commercial because they will get the service that they cannot get at other banks in the area. In fact, it was this basic idea that gave birth to Concord Commercial in the first place. The Bank of Yazoo City can not compete with their giant neighbor on product development or even price. They can, however, compete on service. In fact, they can even dictate the terms of competition by being the outstanding service provider in the market. And by giving its customers higher levels of service than other institutions, the banking side of the business takes care of itself. Cross-selling becomes easier because customers want to buy. Advertising becomes more effective because people believe what they see, and price becomes less of an issue because customers perceive a more value based product/service offering. This single-minded focus of service quality is a theme that we heard over and over at these banks. It is this single-minded focus that makes these banks as successful as they are.

Lesson 10: "Focus on the Relationship, not the Transaction."

Finally, a key lesson is the idea of relationship versus transactional banking. The distinction may be made even more obvious by the fact that several of these outstanding banks think in terms of clients, not customers.

For Concord Commercial Bank this has meant eliminating the structural factors that scream transaction volume. Hawker is quick to point out that his employees spend a lot of time with their clients. They do so at desks, not at teller windows. No one holds a watch on employees to make sure that they are completing the required amount of transactions in a given period of time. Moreover, this makes it easier for the bank employees to know more about their customers and to provide them with other services that can satisfy their banking needs.

Perhaps nowhere, in our experience, is this idea of relationship banking better practiced that at The Northern. Employees are rewarded for establishing relationships with their customers and by sharing the customer with other service departments at the bank. Northern Trust makes a strong concerted and coordinated effort to establish multiple relationships with their clients. In part their focused efforts on personal banking and trust services allow them to do this. But at the heart of this relationship banking, is a solid understanding of what its customers want.

This is a hard concept for many bank managements to grasp. Emphasis has swung to cost reduction and to the use of electronic transactions as a means for greater profitability. The outstanding banks we visited in this book all understand that technology exists to enhance customer service, not to lessen its costs. What may appear to be a mere philosophical quibble is at the heart of this idea of transactional versus relationship banking.

If we bottom-line what we have found in these four organizations that makes them so different from other banks, we would have to point out that these banks have *invested* in a customer service culture. They are committed to the idea that customers will do business with them because the bank will demonstrate the value and importance of the customers to the bank on a daily basis. It cannot be emphasized too strongly that what makes this work is a total commitment to the idea of customer service. To paraphrase Luke Helms' secrets for success:

> This isn't rocket science. It takes hard work. You can tell as many people as you want about what we do at Seafirst. Most of them won't be able to do it because they won't dedicate themselves to making it work!

We echo this sentiment. We have not uncovered any secrets about customer service in these outstanding banks. What we have witnessed is a realization that customer service is the number one strategic imperative for the banking industry during the next decade. Along with this realization is a commitment on the part of these managements to excel in this venue and to make their banks the leading competitors in their markets.

Each bank uses customer service somewhat differently. We hope that you will draw some creative inspiration from reading about these banks and put your bank on the road to becoming the customer service leader in your market.

About the Authors

M. Ray Grubbs, Ph.D.

Dr. Grubbs is Director of the International Business Studies program at Else School of Management, Millsaps College in Jackson, Mississippi. He is also a consultant and has prepared extensive training programs for U.S. and foreign banks. A frequent speaker on banking subjects, Dr. Grubbs has also written the following books: *Winning Banks: Managing Service Quality for Customer Satisfaction, Effective Bank Marketing: Issues, Applications, and Techniques,* and *Developing New Banking Products: A Manager's Guide.*

R. Eric Reidenbach, Ph.D.

Dr. Reidenbach is Professor of Marketing and Director of the Center for Business Development and Research at the University of Southern Mississippi. He consults extensively with the banking industry on such issues as new product development, customer service, and marketing research. A frequent speaker at Bank Administration Institute functions, he is also a lecturer at several banking schools.

Dr. Reidenbach has written several books on bank marketing, including, *Winning Banks: Managing Service Quality for Customer Satisfaction, Bank Marketing: A Guide to Strategic Planning, Effective Bank Marketing: Issues, Applications, and Techniques,* and *Developing New Banking Products: A Manager's Guide.*